P9-CLI-628

Humanitarian Imperialism
Using Human Rights to Sell War

Jean Bricmont

Monthly Review Press
New York

Copyright © 2006 by Jean Bricmont

All Rights Reserved

Library of Congress Cataloging-in-Publication Data

Bricmont, J. (Jean)

[Impérialisme humanitaire. English]

Humanitarian imperialism : using human rights to sell war / by Jean Bricmont; translated by Diana Johnstone

p. cm.

Includes bibliographical references and index.

ISBN 1-58367-147-1 (alk. paper)

1. Humanitarian intervention. 2. Intervention (International law)—History. 3. Humanitarian intervention—Political aspects. 4. Humanitarian intervention—Moral and ethical aspects. 5. Human rights. 6. War—Moral and ethical aspects. I. Title.

KZ6369.B7513 2006

341.5'84—dc22

2006034221

Designed by Terry J. Allen

MONTHLY REVIEW PRESS
146 West 29th street, Suite 6W
New York, NY 10001

Humanitarian Imperialism

Table of Contents

Preface   7

Introduction   17

1. Power and Ideology   29
   Ideological Control in Democratic Societies   31

2. The Third World and the West   35
   The Costs of Imperialism: Direct Victims   37
   The Costs of Imperialism: Killing Hope   38
   The Costs of Imperialism: The Barricade Effect   42
   The Costs of Imperialism: Risks for the Future   52
   The Lesson of Guatemala   58

3. Questions to Human Rights Defenders   61
   The Question of Transition and Development   73
   The Question of Priorities between Types of Rights   83
   The Question of Relationship of Forces
        and Our Position in the World   88

4. Weak and Strong Arguments against War   91

    Weak Arguments   91

    Strong Arguments: The Defense of International Law   93

    Strong Arguments: An Anti-imperialist Perspective   101

5. Illusions and Mystifications   107

    Anti-fascist Fantasies   107

    The European Illusion   112

    The Question of Internationalism   115

    To Sign or Not to Sign Petitions   117

6. The Guilt Weapon   123

    Supporting X   126

    "Neither-Nor"   128

    The Rhetoric of "Support"   134

7. Prospects, Dangers and Hopes   139

    Another Vision of the World Is Possible   139

    Getting Away from Idealism   150

    Imperialism Watch   157

    And As for Hope?   161

Notes   167

Bibliography   181

Index   185

Preface to the English Edition

Two sorts of sentiments inspire political action: hope and indignation. This book is largely the product of the latter sentiment, but the aim of its publication is to encourage the former. A brief and subjective overview of the political evolution of the past twenty years can explain the source of my indignation.

The collapse of the Soviet Union can be compared to the fall of Napoleon. Both were the product of major revolutions whose ideals they symbolized, rightly or wrongly, and which they defended more or less effectively while betraying them in various ways. If their natures were complex, the consequences of their fall were relatively simple and led to a general triumph of reaction, with the United States today playing a role analogous to that of the Holy Alliance nearly two centuries ago.[1] There is no need to be an admirer of the Soviet Union (or of Napoleon) to make this observation. My generation, that of 1968, wanted to overcome the shortcomings of the Soviet system, but certainly did not mean to take the great leap backwards which actually took place and to which, in its overwhelming majority, it has easily adapted.[2] A discussion of the causes of these failures would require several books. Suffice it to say that for all sorts of reasons, some of which will be touched on in what follows, I did not follow the evolution of the majority of my generation and have preserved what it would call my youthful illusions, at least some of them.

And so, when the Kosovo war began in 1999, I found myself completely isolated. To the right, there were still a few *realpolitikers* who saw no good reason for France to wage war against Serbia, least of all to please Germany and the United States. But on the left, the concept of humanitarian intervention was accepted almost unanimously, even within organizations that had retained revolutionary labels, whether Trotskyist, communist, or anarchist. Even today (in August 2006), the movement against the occupation of Iraq is weak and opposition to the threat of war against Iran is weaker still.

In reaction to all that, in 1999 I began writing texts diffused mainly by the Internet, sometimes published here and there. But inasmuch as those texts were often polemic and linked to particular events, I decided, partly in response to various objections encountered in the course of debates, to bring together in a single book my arguments against Western interventionism and its humanitarian justifications. This book was written initially for a European public, but having lived and worked in the United States, I am convinced that it could also be of interest to an American public, for two reasons: for one, because it provides a glimpse of what is going on in Europe, especially in the progressive and ecological circles often idealized by the American left; and for another, because the ideological weaknesses of the movements of opposition to imperial wars are the same on both sides of the Atlantic.

One of the readers of the French edition of this book remarked to me that it was a critique of the left, but one not made from a right-wing viewpoint, which is a fairly good description of what I meant to do. Let us say that the intention here is to make a modest contribution to an ideological reconstruction of the left. Everyone admits that it is weak and, in my view, it is weak, partly because it has not come up with a proper intellectual response to the ideological offensive waged by the right after the fall of communism and has, on the contrary, much too thoroughly interiorized the arguments advanced by the right in the course of that campaign. In this preface, I want to make a few remarks explaining how the arguments made in this book fit into the broader perspective of what could be meant by an intellectual reconstruction of the left.

Historically, one can consider that the "left" represents roughly three types of combat:

- For social control of production, ranging from defense of workers to establishment of different forms of ownership of the means of production other than private.
- For peace, against hegemony, imperialism and colonialism.
- For the defense of democracy, of the rights of the individual, of gender equality, of minorities and of the environment.

Of course, it is perfectly possible to be "on the right" in one of those categories and "on the left" in another. In particular, a good part of the modern right defends "the free market," that is, private ownership of the means of production, while professing moderately "left" positions in the third category mentioned above. Moreover, the isolationist, libertarian or "realistic" right often espouses quite anti-imperialist positions while maintaining views extremely opposed to those of the left on the other points. Besides that, there is a difference betweeen the old left, meaning the communist movement but also most of the rest of the left up until the mid-1960s, which emphasized the first two aspects while underestimating and sometimes completely ignoring the third, and the "new left," which focused its main attention on the third aspect, all too often to the detriment of the first two.

Even if one recognizes the validity of the criticism that the new left addressed to the old left, it is possible to conclude that, on certain problems, the baby has been thrown out with the bathwater. Concerning the first issue, that of social control of the economy, the movement against corporate globalization has been the sign of a reawakening to its fundamental nature. But, when it comes to the subject of this book, the reaction to hegemony and imperialism, the renewal remains feeble, even if the war in Iraq has shown just what sort of disasters result from the intervention policy.

To simplify, one can say that the new left has had the tendency, faced with Western intervention, to waver between two attitudes:

- that which I call humanitarian imperialism, which concedes much too much to the idea that our "universal values" give us the right and even the duty to intervene elsewhere and which opposes imperial wars weakly or not at all. The critique of these ideas is our subject here.

- cultural relativism, that is, the idea that there is no such thing as a moral position having universal value and in whose name one can objectively judge other societies and cultures (or our own).

This second position leads to opposition, on principle, to wars, but it seems to me hard to defend, even if the aim of this book is not to criticize it,[3] but rather to sketch out a third position, which rejects intervention while at the same time accepting as desirable the objectives which it claims to pursue.

In fact, the origin of this debate goes back to the beginning of the colonial era: when the first Europeans arrived in distant lands, they discovered "barbarous customs": human sacrifices, cruel punishments, binding of women's feet, and so on. Violations of human rights, the absence of democracy or the fate of women in Muslim countries are the contemporary version of those barbarous customs. And, confronted with this phenomenon, there have traditionally been three types of reaction in the West. First, that of relativism which denies that there is an objective or universal standard which allows one to say that such customs are barbarous. Second, that of humanitarian imperialism, which uses the denunciation of those customs to legitimatize our interventions, wars and interference. And finally, the point of view that I defend here, which readily admits the barbarous nature of such customs, but considers that our interventions do much.) more harm than good, including in relation to the proclaimed goal of making barbarism recede. And it points out that there is a considerable amount of "barbarism" in our own "civilized" countries, especially when they interact with others. Insofar as the debate, especially in North America, all too often centers on the opposition between "cultural relativists" and "humanitarian imperialists," this third position has a hard time being heard, or even understood for what it is. I hope that this essay, even if it doesn't manage to win readers over to this way of seeing things, will at least help bring it into the debate.

Another problem is that, after the fall of communism, large parts of the left have lost any sense of direction or of purpose or have even entirely given up the very notion of historical progress. To combat that sentiment adequately would require another book, but a few remarks on the history of the 20th century may illustrate the lines along which to proceed.

On July 1, 1916, began the Battle of the Somme; on that single day the British suffered more than 50,000 casualties, out of which 20,000 died. The battle went on for four months, leading to about a million casualties on all sides and the war itself continued for another two years. In the summer of 2006, the Israeli army stopped its attacks on Lebanon after losing about a hundred soldiers; the majority of the U.S. population turned against the Iraq war after fewer than 3,000 died. That indicates a major change in the mentality of the West, and this reluctance to die in large numbers for "God and Country" is major progress in the history of mankind. From the neoconservative point of view, however, this phenomenon is a sign of decadence; in fact one of the positive aspects of the present conflict, from their perspective, is that it should strengthen the moral fiber of the American people, by making them ready to "die for a cause."[4] But, so far, it is not working. More realistic people, the planners at the Pentagon for example, have tried to replace waves of human cannon fodder by massive "strategic" bombing. This works only rarely; in Kosovo and Serbia it did succeed at least in bringing pro-Western clients to power in both places. But it clearly is not enough in Iraq, Afghanistan, Palestine or Lebanon. The only thing that might work, in a very special sense of course, would be nuclear weapons, and the fact that those weapons are the West's last military hope is truly frightening.

To put this observation in a more global context, Westerners do not always appreciate that the major event of the 20th century was neither the rise and fall of fascism, nor the history of communism, but decolonization. One should remember that, about a century ago, the British could forbid the access of a park in Shanghai to "dogs and Chinese." And, of course, most of Asia and Africa was under European control. Latin America was formally independent, but under American and British tutelage; military interventions were routine. All of this collapsed during the 20th century, through wars and revolutions; in fact, the main lasting effect of the Russian Revolution is probably the Soviet Union's not insignificant support to the decolonization process. This process freed hundreds of millions of people from one of the most brutal forms of oppression. It is major progress in the history of mankind, similar to the abolition of slavery in the 18th and 19th centuries.

Still, it is true that the colonial system gave way to the neocolonial one and that most decolonized countries have adopted, at least for the time being, a capitalist form of development. That provides some consolation to the ex-colonialists (and disappoints expectations of the Western left that opposed colonialism). But such sentiments may reflect a misunderstanding of the nature of "socialism" in the 20th century and of the historical significance of the present period. Before 1914, all socialist movements, whether libertarian or statist, reformist or revolutionary, envisioned socialism, that is, the socialization of the means of production, as an historic stage that was supposed to succeed capitalism in relatively developed Western societies possessing a democratic state, a functioning education system and a basically liberal and secular culture. All this disappeared with World War I and the Russian Revolution. After that, the libertarian aspects of socialism withered away, most of the European socialist movements became increasingly incorporated into the capitalist system and its main radical sector, the communists, identified socialism with whatever policies were adopted by the Soviet model. But that model had almost nothing to do with socialism as it was generally understood before the First World War. It should rather be understood as a (rather successful) attempt at rapid economic development of an underdeveloped country, an attempt to catch up, culturally, economically and militarily, by whatever means necessary, with the West. The same is true of post-Soviet revolutions and national liberation movements. As a first approximation, one can say that all over the Third World, people, or rather governments, have tried to "catch up" either by "socialist" or by "capitalist" means.

But, if one recognizes that aspect, the whole history of the 20th century can be interpreted very differently from the dominant discourse about the "socialism that was tried and failed everywhere." What was tried and actually succeeded (almost) everywhere was emancipation from Western domination. This has inverted a centuries-old process of European expansion and hegemony over the rest of the world. The 20th century has not been the one of socialism, but it has been the one of anti-imperialism. And this inversion is likely to continue during the 21st century. Most of the time, the "South" is strengthening itself, with some setbacks (the period surrounding the collapse of the Soviet Union being a time of regression, from that point of view).

This has important consequences for both the Western peace movement and the old issue of socialism. There is some truth to the Leninist idea that the benefits of imperialism corrupt the Western working class—not only in purely economic terms (through the exploitation of the colonies), but also through the feeling of superiority that imperialism has implanted in the Western mind. However, this is changing for two reasons. On the one hand, "globalization" means that the West has become more dependent on the Third World: we do not simply import raw materials or export capital, but we also depend on cheap labor, working either here or in export-oriented factories abroad; we "transfer" capital from the South to the North through "debt payments" and capital flight; and we import an increasing number of engineers and scientists. Moreover, "globalization" means that there is a decrease in linkage between the population of the U.S. and their elites or their capitalists, whose interests are less and less tied to those of "their" country. Whether the population will react by adopting some pro-imperialist fantasies such as Christian Zionism or "the war against terrorism," or whether it will rather increase its solidarity with the emerging countries of the South is a major challenge for the future.

On the other hand, the rise of the South means that there is no longer a preponderance of military force that allows the West to impose its will, the U.S. defeat in Iraq being the most extraordinary illustration of that fact. Of course, there are other means of pressure—economic blackmail, boycotts, buying elections, etc. But countermeasures are increasingly being taken also against those methods, and one should never forget that a relationship of force is always *ultimately* military—without it, how does one get people to pay their debts, for example?

The main error of the communists is to have conflated two notions of "socialism": the one that existed before World War I and the rapid development model of the Soviet Union. But the current situation raises two different questions to which two different forms of "socialism" might be the answer. One is to find paths of development in the Third World, or even a redefinition of what "development" means, that do not coincide with either the capitalist or the Soviet model. But that is a problem to be solved in Latin America, Asia or Africa. In the West, the problem is different: we do not suffer from the lack of satisfaction of basic needs that exists elsewhere (of course, many basic needs are not satisfied, but that is a problem of distribution or of political will rather than one of production or of possibility). The problem here is to define a post-imperialist future for the Western societies, meaning a form of life that would not depend on an unsustainable relation of domination over the rest of the world. Whether one wants to call that "socialism" is a matter of definition, but it would have to include reliance on renewable energy resources, a form of consumption that does not depend on massive imports and an education system that produces the number of qualified people that the nation needs. Whether all this is compatible with the system of private property of the means of production, and a political system largely controlled by those who own those means, remains to be seen.

This establishes a link between the struggle for peace and the struggle for social transformation, because the more we live in peace with the rest of the world, the more we give up our largely illusory military power and stop our constant "threats," the more will we be forced to think about and elaborate an alternative economic order. It is a great tragedy that among Greens, at least among the European ones, this link has been totally lost during the Kosovo and the Afghanistan wars, which most of them supported on humanitarian grounds. It is equally tragic that the opposition to the Iraq war in the United States has been virtually nonexistent and that the population has turned against the war almost entirely as a result of the effectiveness of the Iraqi resistance. As I try to argue in this book, this is partly due to the ideological misrepresentations that have spread widely throughout the left during the period of imperial ideological reconstruction that followed the end of the Vietnam war. The left must clarify its own ideas first and then try to explain to the rest of our societies that we must adapt to an inevitable loss of hegemony. But what I call here humanitarian imperialism is a major obstacle to that enterprise. Yet I don't see any real alternative for the West, except to go back to the spirit of the Battle of the Somme, but this time armed with nuclear weapons.

Acknowledgements

I want to thank Francis McCollum Feeley, professor of American studies at Stendhal University in Grenoble, for giving me the opportunity to present a first version of the ideas developed here at a colloquium that he organized in Grenoble in January 2002 in his research center, the Centre d'études des institutions et des mouvements sociaux américains (CEIMSA).[5] I thank Julie Franck, Edward S. Herman, Anne Morelli, Marie-Ange Patrizio and

Alan Sokal for having read and commented on the preliminary versions of this text. I particularly thank Diana Johnstone for her precious aid and constant support in the preparation of this book. This of course does not imply that they agree with all that is said here.

Introduction

It seems evident, from the attitude of the capitalist world to Soviet Russia, of the Entente to the Central Empires, and of England to Ireland and India, that there is no depth of cruelty, perfidy or brutality from which the present holders of power will shrink when they feel themselves threatened. If, in order to oust them, nothing short of religious fanaticism will serve, it is they who are the prime sources of the resultant evil. ... To make the transition with a minimum of bloodshed, with a maximum of preservation of whatever has value in our existing civilization, is a difficult problem. ... I wish I could think that its solution would be facilitated by some slight degree of moderation and humane feeling on the part of those who enjoy unjust privileges in the world as it is.

—Bertrand Russell[1]

To explain the theme and purpose of this book, let me start by describing a recent encounter with an important representative of the Belgian ecological movement, a woman in the far-left wing of her movement. I reminded her that in the 1980s, at the height of the Cold War when her movement was just getting started, it upheld the idea of a nonviolent civil defense in place of military service, and I asked her how the ecologists came around to the very different positions they have today, for example on the Kosovo war or on the European Union. She replied that pacifism had long since been abandoned, and that she herself would like to see intervention in Africa to put an end to the massive rapes committed there. In the course of the discussion that followed, she told me that she also thought we should intervene to protect the Palestinians and that a preventive war should have been waged against Hitler in the 1930s.

Having taken part in dozens of private and public debates in Belgium, France, Switzerland and Italy ever since the beginning of the new American wars (Yugoslavia, Afghanistan, Iraq), I have repeatedly run into this type of reaction, including, and perhaps primarily, in leftist circles of all shades (ecologists, social democrats, Trotskyists, etc.).[2] Indeed, one of the characteristics of mainstream discourse, from the right to the left, and even going pretty far toward the "extremes" in either direction, is that today's political ethic is totally dominated by what can be called the intervention imperative. Here in Europe we are constantly being called upon to defend the rights of oppressed minorities in remote places (Chechnya, Tibet, Kosovo, Kurdistan), about which as a rule most of us know very little; to protest against violations of human rights in Cuba, China, or Sudan; to call for abolition of the death penalty in the United States; to protect women from persecution in Muslim countries; to support the Palestinian resistance; or perhaps to save the Amazonian forest. The right of humanitarian intervention is not only widely accepted, it often becomes a "duty to intervene." We are told that it is urgent to create international tribunals to judge various crimes committed within the borders of sovereign states. The world is said to have become a global village and we must be involved in everything that goes on everywhere. The wisdom of those who would "mind their own business" is considered anachronistic and reactionary. The left is even more prone to this discourse than the right, and fancies that it is keeping alive the great tradition of working-class internationalism and solidarity with the Spanish Republicans or with anticolonial struggles. Also, denouncing allegedly undemocratic regimes can be considered a way to avoid repeating the "errors of the past," when factions of the left failed to denounce crimes committed by the Soviet Union or were slow to recognize the murderous nature of a self-proclaimed revolutionary Third World movement such as the Khmer Rouge led by Pol Pot (which engaged in massive killings from the time it took power in 1975 until it was overthrown by a Vietnamese intervention, which, ironically, was condemned by Washington).

This web of ideas is rather confused, and one of the main goals of this book will be to try to clarify them. Moreover, these ideas seem to constitute the principal obstacle to building an effective movement of opposition to imperial wars. There was scarcely any visible opposition to the 1999 war against Yugoslavia, the very model of "humanitarian" war, and very little to the war in Afghanistan. It is true that there were huge demonstrations, unique in history and certainly immensely encouraging, against the invasion of Iraq. But it must be admitted that as soon as the Bush administration proclaimed victory, public opinion, at least in the West, fell relatively quiescent, even as the war in Iraq raged on.

~

The United States at War

"America is a nation at war. . . . At the direction of the President, we will defeat adversaries at the time, place, and in the manner of our choosing." Thus opens a recent Pentagon report on the national defense strategy of the United States.[3] Further along, one reads that the United States' leading position in the world continues to breed "unease, a degree of resentment and resistance" and will be challenged by those who employ "a strategy of the weak using international fora, judicial processes, and terrorism" (all lumped together).

~

Meanwhile, starting with the 1999 Seattle demonstrations, a new antiglobalization or "global justice" movement emerged and has developed through various social forums. Its attention has been primarily focused on the economic consequences of neoliberalism, in both the south and north of the planet. The movement has also shown interest in the political and media aspects of domination strategies. But it has paid relatively little attention to their military aspect, and even less to the ideological factors legitimizing military action. But every relationship of domination is, in the last analysis, military, and always needs an ideology as justification.

The ideology of our times, at least when it comes to legitimizing war, is no longer Christianity, nor Kipling's "white man's burden" or the "civilizing mission" of the French Republic, but is a certain discourse on human rights and democracy, mixed in with a particular representation of the Second World War. This discourse justifies Western interventions in the Third World in the name of the defense of democracy and human rights or against the "new Hitlers." This is the discourse and the representation that must be challenged in order to build a radical and self-confident opposition to current and future wars.

The battle of ideas, waged with rigorous reasoning and demystification, is essential to underpin political action. In France, after the end of the decolonization period and the Vietnam War, it was a major ideological offensive waged through the media by the self-styled "new philosophers" that enabled the most conspicuous sector of the French intelligentsia to shift from a somewhat romantic sympathy for the Third World to a growing alignment with U.S. government positions.[4] In the face of current conflicts, an intellectual arsenal is needed in order to challenge mainstream rhetoric and argumentation. We are up against the effects of thirty years of generally well-financed and publicized books, films, lectures, articles and commentaries, endlessly rehashed by the media.

Inasmuch as the intervention discourse is ostensibly an ethical one, it is mainly on ethical grounds that it must be combated. This does not mean that facts are of no importance—they are enormously important—or that the debate is situated on the level of "values," it means that the principal purpose here is not to provide new facts. Facts about U.S. foreign policy are increasingly available, especially thanks to the work of American authors.

What is lacking is a systematic reflection about what those facts imply in regard to our own moral and political responsibilities.

Before opening the debate, let us state some caveats and clear up a few potential misunderstandings. First of all, I have to admit I do not have the means to *prove* my hypothesis; that is, the ideas I criticize are not only very widespread but even, so to speak, constitute the dominant ideology of our times. Quoting this or that author defending those ideas, as I do from time to time, does not constitute proof. Only a long sociological study, which I lack the means to undertake, could establish the facts. Reading elite journals and discussing issues with members of progressive organizations and peace movements have convinced me that the supposed need to defend human rights by military means is indeed the ideological Trojan horse of Western interventionism within the very movements opposed to it in principle—but I don't claim to be able to *prove* this. Certain of my assertions are conjectures rather than certainties, which my situation as an isolated writer without institutional support prevents me from confirming or even studying in greater detail. I nevertheless hope that this discussion of certain ideas will be of interest even to those who are not as convinced as I am of their weight and relevance.

On the other hand, the reader will not find here any analysis, or at least not any very developed analysis, of the internal causes of imperialism, whether economic or of some other order. I shall use the term *imperialism*, though without giving it a "scientific" connotation, to designate Western colonial or neocolonial policies in the Third World. In fact, even if it has more or less fallen out of use, the term seems to me far preferable to the word *empire* which, at least as employed by Hardt, Negri, and their disciples, seems to refer to a vague entity that does not rely on the power of any particular state.

There are many reasons for this refusal to undertake any "profound" analysis of imperialism. Suffice it to say that, for one thing, human phenomena are so complicated and combine so many factors that a reasonable skepticism, such as belongs to the scientific attitude, can lead one to doubt they can be analyzed in a truly scientific way (and not simply proclaimed to be scientific). Of course, it is always possible to select sufficient facts and focus on certain variables so as to give the impression of coming up with a veritable explanation of such-and-such aspects of society or history, but the quite remarkable absence of successful prediction, beyond what plain common sense can come up with, and the rapid obsolescence of such explanations tend to reinforce my skepticism. For another, too little is known about human beings, in particular human motivations, for us to answer certain basic questions: to what extent is man a *homo economicus*, calculating and acting according to his interests and those of his social class, and to what extent is he dominated by "irrational" (from a purely economic viewpoint) passions, such as religion, nationalism, or thirst for power? In the absence of answers to these questions, the real origin of wars and the role of economic factors are difficult to define.

~

Russell on Marx

To desire one's own economic advancement is comparatively reasonable; to Marx, who inherited eighteenth-century rationalist psychology from the British orthodox economists, self-enrichment seemed the natural aim of a man's political actions. But modern psychology has dived much deeper into the ocean of insanity upon which the little barque of human reason insecurely floats. The intellectual optimism of a bygone age is no longer possible to the modern student of human nature. Yet it lingers in Marxism making Marxians rigid and Procrustean in their treatment of the life of instinct. Of this rigidity the materialistic conception of history is a prominent instance.

—Bertrand Russell[5]

~

Turning to possible misunderstandings, one should start by noticing that "third worldist" positions, or even simple criticisms of the West, are increasingly presented as based on some form or other of moral or cultural relativism; in other words, on the idea that it is impossible to make morally objective judgments or, more or less the same, on the notion that their validity is entirely relative to the culture that produced them.

Many critics of imperial policies accept these premises. But they do not apply here. It is perfectly possible to criticize American policies from a universalist—even liberal (in the political and classic sense of the term)—philosophical and conceptual perspective, in the tradition of the Enlightenment. Writers such as Hobson, Twain, Russell, or today Chomsky illustrate this attitude.[6] It can also be noted that criticizing the West in the name of the very values it claims to embody, as I attempt to do here, is simpler and more radical than a relativist critique requiring a preliminary philosophical discussion leading to rejection of the possibility of objective value judgments.

In particular, all the following criticisms of the ideological utilization of human rights in no way challenge the legitimacy of the aspirations contained in the 1948 Universal Declaration of Human Rights. One can be in perfect agreement with certain moral principles and at the same time denounce the way they are misused in practice. Morality is not only a matter of principles; in human relations, as in political discourse, the evocation of principles can very well be a form of hypocrisy, just as self-mortification for crimes for which one is not responsible (those of the past, for example) can serve to gain indulgence toward those for which one is responsible. I might liken my position with respect to human rights to that of left-wing Christians who accept Christian teachings but criticize the way they are used, including by the Church itself, to justify the powers that be. In regard to human rights, the role of the Church is played by leading Western governments, media, and intellectuals, as well as by a certain number of NGOs and progressive movements.

Another misunderstanding to be avoided stems from opposition to imperial wars increasingly being seen as based on strict pacifist principles, or on a philosophy of nonviolence. But that philosophy only becomes relevant in discussing how to react to an *attack*. There is no need to take a position on nonviolence when criticizing wars of aggression, such as the recent American wars. Discussing pacificism or nonviolent defense would be of considerable interest, but it is outside the scope of this book.

Precise definitions of a certain number of terms used rather polemically should help avoid letting the polemics blur the argument. To start with, the term *West* is used to designate a historical and geographical area (the United States and Europe) but will be used mainly to emphasize the ideological fault line between this area and the rest of the world. A detailed study of spontaneous popular reactions to September 11 should suffice to make the point. If I should say, in the Arab world, that instead of attacking Iraq, it would be better to bring the "Zionist entity" (using that term) into line; or, in Latin America and much of Asia, that the very last way to deal with Yugoslavia would be to let the United States exploit that tragedy to legitimatize its unilateral right to intervene, I would not arouse many protests from any part of the political spectrum. In contrast, anyone who makes such remarks in Europe or in the United States will rapidly be drowned out by an indignant chorus of words like Stalin, Pol Pot, anti-Semitism, anti-Americanism—again, right across the political spectrum. This difference illustrates the width and depth of the split.

~

Affluent Egyptians in Cairo Gloat Over Attacks while Eating Big Macs

Sandwiched between a Rolex watch store and a BMW car dealership, the restaurant is packed with affluent university students dressed in American garb and aware of the billions of dollars in foreign aid that the U.S. has pumped into Egypt. It's the sort of place where one would expect to find sympathy for the American cause.

But listen to what they're saying.

Sitting under a poster advertising "Crispy and Delicious McWings," Radwa Abdallah, an 18-year-old university student, is explaining that she rejoiced

when she learned that thousands of Americans had probably died in the terrorist attacks on the World Trade Center and the Pentagon. "Everyone cele-
brated," Ms. Abdallah says, as her girlfriends giggle. "People honked in the
streets, cheering that finally America got what it truly deserved."

Fellow student Raghda El Mahrouqi agrees: "I just hope there were a lot
of Jews in that building," she says. Sherihan Ammar, an aspiring doctor in elaborate makeup and tight T-shirt, sums up her feelings this way: "America was
just too full of itself," she says with a dismissive gesture. . . .

A trip around the capital of Egypt, one of America's main Mideast allies
and the biggest Muslim recipient of U.S. foreign aid, shows that educated, relatively wealthy and seemingly Americanized Arabs just as openly express
their joy at the carnage in the U.S. . . .

Although all Arab governments except Iraq's condemned the U.S. attacks,
the prevailing view even among those horrified by the killings is that what
happened in New York and Washington isn't all that different from what
America itself has inflicted on Iraqis, Palestinians, Sudanese and other Muslims.

More Guarded in Marrakech

Even in thoroughly Western-oriented countries like Morocco, a nation
far removed from the Israeli-Palestinian struggle and a onetime applicant
to join the old European Community, many voice sneaking admiration
for the terrorists. In a convenience store in Er Rachidia, a sand-swept
town at the threshold of the Sahara, the first television images of the
World Trade Center towers engulfed in smoke were greeted with a roar
of approval. "Of course we are happy," says the storekeeper as he invited
a group of foreigners to stop and watch the news.

In Marrakech, the hub of Morocco's tourist industry, reactions were
only a little more guarded. "What happened is a terrible thing for all the
people involved," says Abdou Hamaoui, a 29-year-old civil engineer sip-
ping a glass of lemon Schweppes at the Cafe Glacier on the main square
of the city's old town. "But the U.S. government deserves this." . . .

In an outdoor cafe a short drive away, Ahmed Ahmad Tarif, a 21-year-old business administration student, is wearing a Nike T-shirt. He bought it, he says, because it's good quality, even though he believes that "America stands for racism and for being against freedom and democracy."

Fellow student Ahmed Hussein, bespectacled and with a thin mustache, reflects for a moment when asked about U.S. economic assistance for Egypt. "The money we receive from America and the hatred we feel for America are two separate things," he finally says, "and should not be mixed together."[7]

∼

What I call the "ideology of human rights" will be defined more in detail in chapter 4, but essentially it comes down to the idea that Western states have the right, or the duty, to interfere in the internal affairs of other states in the name of human rights. I use the term "human rights champions" polemically as shorthand for what could be called "self-proclaimed champions of human rights" or "those who base their political action primarily on human rights ideology."

Finally, in criticizing a power and its legitimization mechanisms, it is one thing to denounce its *hypocrisy* and quite another to point to the disastrous human *consequences* of the exercise of power. These are two different things, even if a persistently hypocritical power cannot generally be expected to produce positive results. Even if, as I try to show, the hypocrisy goes deeper than what is usually recognized by the critics, that is not the essential point of my argument, which is mainly concerned with the *consequences* of imperialism.

My principal aim is to challenge the good conscience that prevails in the West and the ideological convictions that uphold it, and to open a debate within peace, ecological, and progressive movements. If what one wants is a peace policy, the very first thing that must be done is to try to understand others, including the "enemy"—all the more if his reactions are aggressive or irrational. The "war without end" against terrorism gives no sign of being simply a war of short and joyous conquests. And if powerful Western states are repeatedly attacked at home by terrorists, it is to be seriously feared that "the little barque of human reason" may well capsize into the "ocean of insanity"—unless we are willing to radically change our way of envisioning our relations with the rest of the world.

1

Power and Ideology

Whenever dictators, monarchs, bosses, aristocrats, bureaucrats, or colonialists exercise power over others, they need a justifying ideology. That justification almost always comes down to the same formula: when A exercises power over B, he does so for B's "own good." In short, power habitually presents itself as altruistic. In 1815, at the fall of Napoleon, the tsar of Russia, the Austrian emperor, and the king of Prussia came together in what they called their Holy Alliance, claiming to base "their reciprocal relations upon the sublime truths which the Holy Religion of our Savior teaches" as well as on "the precepts of that Holy Religion, namely, the precepts of Justice, Christian Charity, and Peace," and vowed to regard "themselves toward their subjects and armies as fathers of families." During the Boer War, the British prime minister, Lord Salisbury, declared that it was "a war for democracy," and that "we seek no goldfields, we seek no territory." Bertrand Russell, citing these remarks, commented that "cynical foreigners noted that we nevertheless got both goldfields and territory."[1] Hitler, for his part, waged his wars to protect (German) minorities and defend Europe from Bolshevism.

At the height of the Vietnam War, the American historian Arthur Schlesinger described U.S. policy there as part of "our general program of international good will."[2] At the end of that war, a liberal commentator wrote in the *New York Times*: "For a quarter-century, the United States has been trying to do good, encourage liberty and promote social justice in the Third World." But, in doing so, "we have been living beyond our moral resources and have fallen into hypocrisy."[3] It is fairly difficult to find an openly cynical power; individuals living on the margins of society, such as members of street gangs or mafias, no doubt provide the best examples.

But this nearly universal altruism in the legitimization discourse is precisely what ought to arouse skepticism. Indeed, that is exactly what happens in daily life: altruistic statements are commonly greeted with skepticism and with reminders that acts speak louder than words. Yet in public life, words often manage to outweigh acts.

~

What We're Fighting For: A Letter from America

We pledge to do all we can to guard against the harmful temptations— especially those of arrogance and jingoism—to which nations at war so often seem to yield. At the same time, with one voice we say solemnly that it is crucial for our nation and its allies to win this war. We fight to defend ourselves, but we also believe that we fight to defend those universal principles of human rights and human dignity that are the best hope for humankind.

One day, this war will end. When it does—and in some respects even before it ends—the great task of conciliation awaits us. We hope that this war, by stopping an unmitigated global evil, can increase the possibility of a world community based on justice. But we know that only the peacemakers among us in every society can ensure that this war will not have been in vain.

We wish especially to reach out to our brothers and sisters in Muslim societies. We say to you forthrightly: We are not enemies, but friends. We must not be enemies. We have so much in common. There is so much that we must do together. Your human dignity, no less than ours—your rights and opportunities for a good life, no less than ours—are what we believe we're fighting for. We know that, for some of you, mistrust of us is high, and we know that we Americans are partly responsible for that mistrust. But we must not be enemies. In hope, we wish to join with you and all people of good will to build a just and lasting peace.[4]

~

Ideological Control in Democratic Societies

Ideology is especially important in democratic societies, where it may constitute the principal form of social control. The dominant ideology is far more powerful in the United States, with its freedom of expression, than it was in the Soviet Union, where the obvious monopoly of political expression, enforced by repression, created widespread disbelief. In more autocratic societies, people are kept in line by fear. In a society where people are free to demonstrate and vote, control over "hearts and minds" needs to be much deeper and more constant.

The enforcement of mainstream ideology in our societies is the task of what has been called the secular priesthood, an analogy for the religious priesthood in traditional societies.[5] That traditional priesthood presented itself as an intermediary between the human and the divine and legitimized the power of the dominant social strata by appropriate interpretation of divine will. In so doing, it ensured its own relatively privileged social position under protection of the temporal power.

With the Enlightenment and the democratic revolutions in Europe, the role of religion as a justification for power was constantly eroded. Lord Salisbury's remarks about democracy cited above have a more contemporary ring than those of the Holy Alliance about religion. Even someone as ostentatiously religious as George W. Bush does not justify his wars primarily in the name of religion, but rather in the name of democracy and human rights. It is worth noting that his supporters in Europe are often embarrassed by his religious side and wish that he would stick strictly to the human rights discourse.

Today's secular priesthood is made up of opinion makers, media stars of all kinds, and a considerable number of academics and journalists. They largely monopolize public debate, channelling it in certain directions and setting the limits on what can be said, while giving the impression of a free exchange of ideas. One of the most common ideological reinforcement mechanisms is to focus debate on the *means* employed to achieve the supposedly altruistic ends claimed by those in power, instead of asking whether the proclaimed aims are the real ones, or whether those pursuing them have the right to do so. To take a current example, the question will be debated as to whether the United States has the means and intelligence to impose democracy on the Middle East, or, eventually, whether the price to pay (the war) is not too high. All these debates only reinforce the idea that the proclaimed intentions (to liberate peoples, to spread democracy) are the real ones and that less noble consequences, such as control of oil or strengthening American hegemony (globally) and Israeli hegemony (locally) are only collateral effects of a generous enterprise.

~

Bush's Loyal Opposition

In a speech to the Veterans of Foreign Wars in Chicago on January 10, 2006, President George W. Bush said he welcomed "honest critics" who question the way the war is being conducted and the "loyal opposition" that points out what is wrong with his administration's approach. But he termed irresponsible the "partisan critics who claim that we acted in Iraq because of oil or because of Israel or because we misled the American people," as well as "defeatists who refuse to see that anything is right."

~

It is very important to those in power to confine public debate within the narrow limits of whether or not means and tactics are effective, which leave unchallenged the nature and legitimacy of aims and strategies. In an autocratic society, such debates would not be allowed. In our societies, they are actually quite useful. The "respectable" left plays a major role in this legitimization process by focusing debate on the first type of questions (means and effectiveness) and marginalizing the second (the nature and legitimacy of ends). In contrast, we can expect that any analysis of past or adversary powers, such as the Roman Empire, Napoleon, or the Soviet Union, will include a critical look at their legitimization mechanisms, without accepting at face value their official declarations of purpose. It is only when speaking of *our* societies *today* that such analysis is considered out of line.

Another ideological reinforcement mechanism frequently used by the respectable left is the ritual denunciation of "totalitarian" systems of indoctrination, usually with almost religious reference to Orwell, in particular concerning characteristic features of systems least like our own. This encourages the notion that mechanisms to control and manipulate people's minds are to be found everywhere except in our own societies.

On the other hand, when critics of our system, such as the communists in the past, claim that it is not fundamentally different from totalitarian systems, they are easily refuted, since the mere freedom to express such criticism is enough to show the difference. That line of criticism only helps to blur understanding of how ideological control works here and now, by giving the impression that the only indoctrination mechanisms are those which are not found in our societies.

It is important to note that ideology is not the same thing as lies. Members of the secular priesthood usually believe what they say. Indeed, their internalization of ideology is essential for them to be effective. This shows up in the obvious contrast between the way they express themselves and the dull ritualistic discourse of those who repeat an ideology they don't really believe.

When it comes to individuals who really have power, political or economic, the matter is a bit more complicated, but even there, the hypothesis of generalized cynicism is not plausible. Ideology has the advantage of enabling people to live in a state of mental comfort where they can avoid asking troubling questions. This means that criticizing the lack of sincerity of those in power or of the secular priesthood should be done with precision: the problem is not that they are lying or that they are consciously hiding their real aims, but that they spontaneously adopt a distorted view of the world and history that enables them to profit from their privileged position with a perfectly clear conscience. This is a phenomenon that can be observed in daily life: generous words and speeches about "values" often go hand in hand with an analysis of reality that conveniently makes it possible to identify personal interest with moral imperatives. Genuine sincerity is not simply a matter of believing what one says, but of honestly asking whether the actions one undertakes really serve the noble aims one claims to pursue. Unfortunately, there is nothing new about all this, and those who criticize the organization of society today, in one way or another, have a lot in common with Blaise Pascal or Jonathan Swift criticizing the injustice and hypocrisy of society in their day.

However banal this may be, it is nevertheless important because it implies that ideological representations of the world, since they are not simply lies, may have unforeseen results and can sometimes, if defended with enough fanaticism, actually have harmful consequences for the very powers they are supposed to legitimize. It is still too soon to say whether the American attack on Iraq is an example of such a situation, but the German invasion of the Soviet Union in 1941, as well as the obstinate American war in Vietnam— both of which claimed to aim at "liberating peoples from communism"—are both clear examples of pursuing ideological aims all the way to disaster.

2

The Third World and the West

With the end of the decolonization process, the suggestion of any conflict beween the Third World and the West has been increasingly dismissed as out of date. The mainstream discourse stresses that the Third World is by no means united and that many of its leaders (or the domestic opposition to its leaders) have abandoned their earlier nationalism in favor of pro-Western liberalism. Nevertheless, it remains true that an ongoing conflict exists, at least in a latent form, just as class conflicts can take more or less antagonistic forms from one historical period to another. There is conflict concerning the terms of trade, debt, provisions of raw materials—conflict that can very well explode into open hostilities, as in the Gulf wars. Moreover, both in Latin America and in the Muslim world (despite the sharp differences between those two regions), the vision of relations between "us" and "them" is very different from ours. In general, that vision is dismissed as stemming from fanaticism or jealousy, especially in the case of the Muslims.

Let us start, then, by summarizing what can be considered wrong with Western interventions in the Third World from a universalist point of view, without going back to the African slave trade and other past horrors of colonialism, rather focusing on the policies pursued since 1945, especially by the

United States. These have given imperialism its neocolonial form. Countries remain formally independent, but every form of coercion is brought to bear to keep them under Western domination. If we examine those policies objectively we should be able to grasp the answer to that famous post–September 11 question, "Why do they hate us?" We should be able to understand why it would be perfectly natural, if not to hate "us," at least to hate the policies pursued by our governments. And then we can also understand why we would no doubt feel the same as they do if we were in their place.

The costs of Western imperialism to the Third World can be divided into four different categories.

～

A Dangerous Example

The United States supported the brutal Somoza dictatorship in Nicaragua for over forty years. The Nicaraguan people, led by the Sandinistas, overthrew this regime in 1979, a breathtaking popular revolution. The Sandinistas weren't perfect. ... But they were intelligent, rational, and civilized. They set out to establish a stable, decent, pluralistic society. The death penalty was abolished. ... More than 100,000 families were given title to land. Two thousand schools were built. A quite remarkable literacy campaign reduced illiteracy in the country to less than one-seventh. Free education was established and a free health service. Infant mortality was reduced by a third. Polio was eradicated. The United States denounced these achievements as Marxist-Leninist subversion. In the view of the U.S. government, a dangerous example was being set. ...

The United States finally brought down the Sandinista government. It took some years and considerable resistance but relentless economic persecution and 30,000 dead finally undermined the spirit of the Nicaraguan people. They were exhausted and poverty-stricken once again. The casinos moved back into the country. Free health and free education were over. Big business returned with a vengeance. "Democracy" had prevailed.

But this "policy" was by no means restricted to Central America. It was conducted throughout the world.... The United States supported and in many cases engendered every right-wing military dictatorship in the world after the end of the Second World War. I refer to Indonesia, Greece, Uruguay, Brazil, Paraguay, Haiti, Turkey, the Philippines, Guatemala, El Salvador, and, of course, Chile. ... Hundreds of thousands of deaths took place throughout these countries.... Even while it was happening it wasn't happening. It didn't matter. It was of no interest. The crimes of the United States have been systematic, constant, vicious, remorseless, but very few people have actually talked about them. ...

I believe that despite the enormous odds which exist, unflinching, unswerving, fierce intellectual determination, as citizens, to define the real truth of our lives and our societies is a crucial obligation which devolves upon us all. It is in fact mandatory. If such a determination is not embodied in our political vision we have no hope of restoring what is so nearly lost to us—the dignity of man.

—Harold Pinter, 2005 Nobel Prize Lecture

∼

The Costs of Imperialism: Direct Victims

To start with, let us consider the wars waged by the United States. They have killed millions of people, especially in Korea, Indochina, Central America, and Iraq. To that death toll must be added the victims of their protégés: Suharto, Mobutu, Pinochet; the Argentinian, Guatemalan, and Brazilian military regimes; the rebel groups supported by the United States and South Africa in Angola and Mozambique; and, finally, Israel. The author William Blum has called this the "American holocaust."[1] The expression may be shocking, but what ought to be much more shocking is the relative indifference in the face of those crimes and that they are seldom perceived as the result of a systematic policy. The impact of the Rwandan tragedy or of Hiroshima on public consciousness is no doubt due to the fact that each of these slaughters took place within a short period of time. But if a system of domination regularly produces so much death and suffering, is the horror any less just because it stretches over a longer period of time? Shouldn't it be surprising that in the post-1945 world, where racism was officially discredited and abolished, people who consider themselves civilized have killed so many people they consider not civilized enough? The American system of domination is not the first to cost countless lives. But unlike those of the past, the American system is functioning now, and we can oppose it, whereas there is nothing we can do for victims of the past.

Killing Hope

The real problem goes much deeper. It is an understatement to say that it amounts to a loss of opportunity for the Third World. Today the slogan "Another world is possible" is widely taken up by critics of economic globalization. But if it is true today, why wasn't it true yesterday? Let us try to imagine such a world. A world in which Congo, Cuba, Vietnam, Brazil, Chile, Iraq, Guatemala, and many other countries would have been able to develop without constant interference from the West. A world in which secular movements in the Arab world could have continued to modernize the Middle East without having to fight on two fronts, between aggressively "modern" Zionism and feudal obscurantism, both supported by Western powers. A world in which apartheid would have been overcome long ago, avoiding the disasters and wars it provoked.

Of course, such "another world" would not be heaven on earth. There would no doubt still be civil wars, massacres, and famines. But the West is no paradise, either, and least of all during the period of its own modernization, with children working in mines, semi-slaves working in the colonies, and tens of millions killed in the two great European civil wars known as the First and Second World Wars. Nevertheless, it is hard to believe that the situation would not have been better had Third World countries been allowed to pursue their own ways of developing instead of being subjected to leaders imposed by the West. Compare, in terms of intelligence, humanity, and honesty, the leaders "they" produced and those that the West supported against them: Arbenz and the Guatemalan dictators, Sukarno and Suharto, Lumumba and Mobutu, the Sandinistas and Somoza, Goulart and the Brazilian generals, Allende and Pinochet, Mandela and apartheid, Mossadegh and the Shah, and today, Chávez and the Venezuelan putschists.[2]

Think also of the positive influence successful public health and land reform policies could have had on other poor countries if those experiments in China or in Cuba, but also elsewhere—for example in Guatemala in the early 1950s—had not run up against constant hostility from the West. If one thinks about it, and even if it is impossible to make a precise calculation, one can realize that Western obstruction of such progressive measures has cost not millions but hundreds of millions of lives destroyed by hunger, disease, and poverty. To give a simple example, in 1989 the economists Jean Drèze and Amartya Sen estimated that, starting from similar basic conditions, China and India followed different paths of development and that the difference between the social systems of the two countries (notably in regard to health care) resulted in 3.9 million more deaths annually in India. This means that "India seems to manage to fill its cupboard with more skeletons every eight years than China put there in its years of shame," 1958 to 1961. Of course, the Chinese famines are regularly blamed on communism, but it would not occur to anybody to blame the extra Indian deaths on capitalism or democracy.[3]

Latin America and the Cuban Difference

In Cuba, life expectancy is six years longer than the rest of the continent. Under-five mortality is four times below the average. If Latin America could show the same results as Cuba, 250,000 children's lives could be saved every year.[4] There are 5.7 million working children in Latin America.[5] For the whole continent, there are 50 million street children.[6] None of these situations are to be found in Cuba, where all children go to school.

∼

I should point out that this criticism is independent of whatever can be said about old-style colonialism. The latter was even more violent than contemporary imperialism, but it indirectly helped to spread medical and scientific knowledge, as well as certain liberal and democratic ideas in places where they did not yet exist. This is not to suggest that the tens of millions of deaths brought about by colonialism can be justified by that spread of ideas, which might have been accomplished otherwise. What needs to be stressed here is that the present situation is radically different. American policy has very often been directed against movements that were essentially "modernizing"; for example, those that emerged from the Bandung Conference and merely sought to enable their own societies to benefit from the advantages of science and, in some cases, of democracy.[7] It should also be noted that the policies of democratically elected presidents Allende of Chile and Arbenz of Guatemala were in reality scarcely more radical than those of the Swedish social democrats after 1931 or the British Laborites after 1945. But they ran up against incomparably greater foreign-backed opposition.

To defeat such progressive movements, Western powers have often supported the most feudal and obscurantist tendencies, for example, in Angola, Afghanistan or Indochina. Finally, the very fact that the West engages in pillage of resources and massive support for Israel at the same time it presents itself as the champion of modernity and enlightenment tends only to discredit those ideas, particularly in the Muslim world. The selfishness and short-sightedness of Western policymakers weaken the appeal of the universal ideas they claim to defend so ardently.

∼

But We Changed

America's empire is not like empires of times past, built on colonies, conquest and the white man's burden. We are no longer in the era of the United Fruit Company, when American corporations needed the Marines to secure their investments overseas. The 21st century imperium is a new invention in the annals of political science, an empire lite, a global hegemony whose grace notes are free markets, human rights and democracy, enforced by the most awesome military power the world has ever known. It is the imperialism of a people who remember that their country secured its independence by revolt against an empire, and who like to think of themselves as the friend of freedom everywhere. It is an empire without consciousness of itself as such, constantly shocked that its good intentions arouse resentment abroad. But that does not make it any less of an empire, with a conviction that it alone, in Herman Melville's words, bears "the ark of the liberties of the world."

—Michael Ignatieff [8]

Or, did we?

Of course, the apologists for every other imperial power have said the same thing. So you can go back to John Stuart Mill, one of the most outstanding Western intellectuals, now we're talking about the real peak of moral integrity and intelligence. He defended the British Empire in very much those words. John Stuart Mill wrote the classic essay on humanitarian intervention. Everyone studies it in law schools. What he says is, Britain is unique in the world. It's unlike any country before it. Other countries have crass motives and seek gain and so on, but the British act only for the benefit of others.

—Noam Chomsky [9]

Or should one believe this?

The hidden hand of the market will never work without the hidden fist—McDonald's cannot flourish without McDonnell Douglas, the designer of the F-15. And the hidden fist that keeps the world safe for Silicon Valley's technologies is called the United States Army, Air Force, Navy and Marine Corps.

—Thomas L. Friedman[10]

≈

The Barricade Effect

When human beings are attacked, they often tend not only to defend themselves but to do so in an excessive and irrational manner; for example, by hunkering down and cutting themselves off from the rest of the world, which often only increases the dangers from which they seek to protect themselves. Almost everyone seemed to understand that tendency when it came to American reactions to September 11: yet this led to the invasion and occupation of two countries, hundreds of thousands of people killed, and, in addition to all that, exaggerated security measures bordering on the absurd. But just suppose that an event comparable to September 11 took place on American soil every day for ten years. What would be the reaction? How many million people would be killed in retaliation? What would become of the famous democratic freedoms of which Americans are so proud? How many people would be unceremoniously thrown into what Amnesty International already calls the "American gulag"—Guantánamo and other more obscure camps? However, the total number of casualties caused by that hypothetical series of events would be on a scale comparable to the loss of human life suffered by the Soviet Union during the Second World War, or even during the course of the civil war that followed the 1917 revolution, when the counterrevolution was supported by Western military intervention.[11]

Yet throughout the Cold War, very few in the West understood that a large part of Soviet policy, including its control over Eastern Central Europe, far from being aggressive and aiming at world hegemony, was, on the contrary, excessively and clumsily defensive and, in the face of the danger of another aggression from the West, relatively moderate, at least in comparison to American wars after September 11. The risk of Western aggression, even if it was not as great as it looked to Soviet leaders after 1945, was nevertheless more real than the danger of communism brandished in Europe at the same time, or the danger of Islamism brandished today. The same thing could be said for a good part of the spy mania and the repression that flourished in the USSR. In the mainstream Western discourse, these evils are attributed to a purely internal cause, Stalinism. But no one can say what would have happened if the Soviet Union had not been born in the horrors of civil war and had not felt obliged, lucidly enough, to catch up with the West industrially and militarily in the space of a decade to confront the Nazi threat. One can scarcely expect a society subjected to such violence to become a model of humanism, moderation, and democracy.

The leftist discourse on the Soviet Union, especially on the part of Trotskyists, anarchists, and a majority of contemporary communists, usually fails to recognize that aspect of things in its eagerness to denounce Stalinism. But insofar as a large part of Stalinism can be considered a reaction to external attacks and threats (imagine again a regular series of September 11 attacks on the United States), the denunciation amounts to a defense of imperialism that is all the more pernicious for adopting a revolutionary pose.

I know from experience that the usual answer to such objections is to say that such factors "don't explain everything" and that one cannot "justify the unjustifiable," that is, Stalinism. One encounters similar reactions when observing that the particularly vengeful way the First World War was concluded through the Versailles Treaty was one of the origins of Nazism, or suggesting that perhaps the terrorist attacks on New York, Madrid, or

London were not unrelated to Western policies in Iraq and Palestine.[12] Let us examine those objections.

In regard to what is or is not "justifiable," we must choose between two fundamentally opposite attitudes toward ethical questions. One of them, which could be called "religious"—even if it does not always stem from the notion of a personal god—and which is strongly expressed both by the French "new philosophers" and in the speeches of George W. Bush, is that Good and Evil exist and do battle in and by themselves, that is, independently of any given historical circumstances. The "bad guys"—Hitler, Stalin, Osama bin Laden, Milosevic, Saddam, etc.—are demons that emerge from nowhere, effects without causes. To combat Evil, the only solution is to mobilize what is Good: arouse it from its lethargy, arm it, and send it off to destroy Evil. That is the philosophy of permanent good conscience and of war without end.

The opposite viewpoint, which can be called "materialist" or "scientific," attempts to situate tragedies and crimes, great or small, in the chain of cause and effect. This is not a matter of denying free will, that is, freedom to make good and evil choices, but rather to leave to one side the seemingly unanswerable question of whether or not human beings are "really" free—and if so, under what circumstances—and to consider that it is only by understanding and acting on causes that one can combat the effects (evil). In Europe, at least, this conception is today almost universally accepted in regard to ordinary criminality. But this is far from the case when it comes to historical tragedies and relations between states. Nevertheless, international law and most efforts in pursuit of peace are related to that philosophy. It also has the merit of encouraging a sense of modesty and a critical mind, and, in regard to our subject, of raising the question as to what it is in Western policy that provokes despair and violent reactions. This is more useful than throwing up our hands and denouncing evil when unexpected events occur.

As for the comment, "But that doesn't explain everything," it would certainly be absurd to see Stalinism, Nazism, or Islamic terrorism as solely the result of external actions such as civil war, the Versailles Treaty, or occupation of Palestine and Iraq. All those social phenomena have complex causes, and no truly scientific analysis is capable of determining which are the most important. There are obviously internal factors. In the case of the American reaction to September 11, or to what would be a series of such attacks, among such internal factors there is a national self-righteousness far greater than in most other countries.

The mainstream discourse (at least among the United States and its allies) presents the American reaction as "normal," given the dangers, whereas the reaction of the Soviet Union in the past and of the Muslim world today is presented as irrational and unconnected to any threat. But human beings everywhere display excessive defensive reactions and not very pretty desires for vengeance. If we want to be honest, the first thing to do is to look at others in the same way we would look at ourselves.

∼

Western Policy toward the Russian Revolution

Every failure of industry, every tyrannous regulation brought about by the desperate situation, is used by the Entente as a justification of its policy. If a man is deprived of food and drink, he will grow weak, lose his reason, and finally die. This is not usually considered a good reason for inflicting death by starvation. But where nations are concerned, the weakness and struggles are regarded as morally culpable, and are held to justify further punishment. … Is it surprising that professions of humanitarian feeling on the part of English people are somewhat coldly received in Soviet Russia?

—Bertrand Russell[13]

∼

Today, people in the West, especially the more hawkish, boast of winning the Cold War, which is most often attributed to American intransigence under Reagan than to European policies of compromise such as Willy

Brandt's Ostpolitik, and hope that a similarly intransigent attitude will
bring them victory in the "war against terror." But it may be suggested that
the relative incapacity of the Soviet system to reform itself was partly due to
the constant feeling of being under threat, a feeling fostered by Western
aggression. The "conservatives" within the system could always argue that
Stalin's leadership did at least finally result in victory, peace, and security.
When the system finally collapsed, it did so in a way that had catastrophic
consequences for the living standards of a large part of its population.
There is reason to think that a more gradual evolution, facilitated by less
external pressure and which had already begun under Khrushchev, could
have been much easier on the population. George Kennan, the father of the
U.S. containment (of Soviet communism) policy, stated in 1992 that "the
general effect of Cold War extremism was to delay rather than hasten the
great change that overtook the Soviet Union."[14]

~

Socialism and the West

In the former Soviet republics, the decline in life expectancy has been spectacular, especially among men. In the Russian Federation, average life expectancy of men has gone from 70 years in the mid-1980s to 59 years and is today
lower than in India. This situation is due notably to economic collapse, decline
in the social welfare system and the prevalence of alcoholism and illness.
Nontransmissible illnesses such as cardiovascular disease and injuries
account for the greater part of the increase in deaths, although infectious dis-
eases are also recurrent. If this death rate remains stable, 40 percent of boys
age 15 today will die before the age of 60 in Russia.[15]

~

The same type of reflection applies to most formerly colonized countries.
There is no telling what would have become of Algeria, Vietnam, Korea,
China, the Middle East, without the destruction of war, the imposed opium

trade, the occupation of Palestine, the Sykes-Picot Accords, Suez, etc.[16] Revolutionary violence can repeatedly be shown to be the product rather than the cause of counterrevolutionary violence, as well as of long-lasting oppression by traditional ruling classes and foreign invasions.[17]

Moreover, if it is true, as often said, that most socialist regimes turn out to be dictatorships, that is largely because a dictatorship is much harder to overthrow or subvert than a democracy. It follows that the repeated assaults by the Western ruling classes against every form of socialism have provoked a sort of artificial selection that allows only dictatorial forms to survive. After successfully ousting the democratically elected Mossadegh from power in Iran, the CIA agent Kermit Roosevelt tried to mount a similar putsch in Syria, but failed because Syria was already a dictatorship.[18] Castro has survived in Cuba long after the fall of Allende in Chile.

~

The Overthrow of Mossadegh

In 1953, the CIA organized a coup d'état that succeeded in overthrowing the government of Muhammed Mossadegh, a conservative nationalist who sought to wrest control of Iranian petroleum from the Anglo-American companies for the benefit of his own country. Celebrating the event, the *New York Times* wrote in its August 6, 1954, editorial: "Underdeveloped countries with rich resources now have an object lesson in the heavy cost that must be paid by one of their number which goes berserk with fanatical nationalism. It is perhaps too much to hope that Iran's experience will prevent the rise of other Mossadeghs in other countries, but that experience may at least strengthen the hands of more reasonable and more far-seeing leaders."[19]

~

Even though socialism is not the topic under discussion here, one can argue that far from having "failed wherever it was tried," it has not really been tried anywhere. Wherever radical social changes have occurred, they could only take place in such violent circumstances as to rule out any possibility of socialism, that is, of what was understood by the term in the European socialist movement of the nineteenth century up until the outbreak of the First World War in 1914: overcoming the injustices of the capitalist system by collective appropriation of the means of production in such a way as to preserve "all that is valuable in existing civilization," as Russell put it, in particular the benefits of peace and democracy. A main source of the tragedies of the twentieth century is that the war waged from 1914 to 1918 brought to power those socialists most inclined to use the weapon of dictatorship, the Bolsheviks, and doomed the others to marginalization, or even death (Jean Jaurès, Karl Kautsky, Rosa Luxemburg), leading to a polemical polarization between communists and social democrats that drowned out reasonable voices of intellectuals such as Bertrand Russell.[20] This role of the war in distorting socialism is usually overlooked by those who speak of the horrors of the twentieth century because it argues against war, which is the exact opposite of the "lessons of history" drawn by those who advocate preventive war to eliminate dictatorships and spread democracy.

This line of thought also provides answers to those who advocate Western interventionism by referring to the crimes of Pol Pot or to massacres in Rwanda and Srebrenica. Those tragedies, it is claimed, would have justified military interventions that unfortunately did not take place due to our lack of courage or pressure from anti-imperialist movements. But all three of these tragedies can be shown to have in part resulted from previous interventionist policies. In Cambodia, it is scarcely plausible that the Khmer Rouge would have come to power had the United States not dragged the country into its war by massive "secret" bombing and overthrown Prince Sihanouk to install a dictator of its choice.[21] As for Rwanda, first German and then Belgian colonial rule played on the principle of "divide and rule," setting Tutsis and Hutus against each other. Should Iraq be plunged into full-fledged civil war between Shiites, Sunnis, and Kurds, one can count on Western humanitarians to shake their heads in dismay at the "barbarity" of those peoples, locked in their primitive religious and nationalist cultures, while forgetting all that the Americans have done, whether deliberately or by ignorant arrogance, to set them at one another's throats.

Curiously, there have been far fewer calls for intervention in Eastern Congo, where there have been massacres apparently as bloody, or even more so, than in Rwanda. The explanation may be that the hypothetical solution in Rwanda would have been a U.S. or Western intervention, which is the course of action that mainstream discourse seeks to legitimize, whereas in Congo, it might well have sufficed to demand the withdrawal of Rwandan and Ugandan troops to end the conflict. Such a demand would have been in perfect conformity with international law and might have shown the latter's efficacy rather than its weakness. The Rwanda of Paul Kagame and its ally Uganda are certainly not great powers, but they are favored clients of the United States, unlike the first Kabila government of Congo at the time of their incursions. This may explain why the death and destruction in Eastern Congo in the 1990s failed to arouse the massive indignation of Western media and humanitarian warriors.

The Srebrenica massacre has become the argument par excellence in favor of unilateral intervention and the symbol of the alleged failure of the United Nations. A great deal could be said about this. Suffice it here to remark on the origins of the war in Bosnia, toward the end of which the massacre took place. After all, if one wants to avoid massacres committed during wars, one should first ask how to prevent wars. Now, just before that war broke out, negotiations had taken place to reach an agreement on the "cantonization" of Bosnia-Hezegovina. As the journalist Diana Johnstone writes:

> The cantonization proposal was signed on March 18, 1992, by Izetbego-
> vic, Karadzic and Boban on behalf of the Muslim, Serb and Croat commu-
> nities respectively. It was accepted by all three parties as a compromise to
> avoid civil war. The Serbs and Croats accepted recognition of independent
> Bosnia-Herzegovina within existing boundaries, which they did not want,

in exchange for "cantonization," which the Muslim party did not want. The compromise did not satisfy Mr. Izetbegovic because (in the words of United States Ambassador to Yugoslavia Warren Zimmermann) it would have "denied him and his Muslim party a dominant role in the republic." Ambassador Zimmermann hastened to call on Mr. Izetbegovic in Sarajevo to discuss the Lisbon accord. "He said he didn't like it, I told him, if he didn't like it, why sign it?" Zimmermann recalled later. Apparently only too glad to be encouraged to hold out for more, Izetbegovic reversed himself and withdrew his support for the Lisbon accord.

"What was the full intent or effect of the U.S. ambassador's remark? Opinions differ. The fact remains that the same United States ambassador who first prohibited the Yugoslav People's Army from maintaining the unity of Yugoslavia, then went on to encourage Izetbegovic's party to fight to maintain the unity of Bosnia-Herzegovina. Morally and practically, this was contradictory. Practically it made no sense at all: the Yugoslav People's Army, if not opposed by NATO powers, would have been able to hold Yugoslavia together, obliging the parties thereafter to reach peaceful accommodation. Izetbegovic's Muslim forces, in contrast, while stronger than admitted, were clearly not able to hold Bosnia-Herzegovina together without considerable outside military assistance."[22]

~

The Lisbon Agreements

For instance, of the Lisbon agreements of February 1992, the Canadian Ambassador to Yugoslavia at the time, James Bissett, has written, "The entire diplomatic corps was very happy that the civil war had been avoided— except the Americans. The American Ambassador, Warren Zimmerman, immediately took off for Sarajevo to convince [the Bosnian Muslim leader] Izetbegovic not to sign the agreement." Zimmerman later admitted this, although he claimed, implausibly, just to be helping Izetbegovic out of an agreement with which the latter was uncomfortable. However, according to "a high-ranking State Department official who asked not to be identified," quoted in the New York Times, "The policy was to encourage Izetbegovic to break the partition plan. It was not committed to paper." That was Bush Sr. As for Clinton, in February 1993 David Owen made this public statement:

> Against all the odds, even against my own expectations we have more or less got a settlement but we have a problem. We can't get the Muslims on board. And that's largely the fault of the Americans, because the Muslims won't budge while they think Washington may come into it on their side any day now. . . . It's the best settlement you can get, and it's a bitter irony to see the Clinton people block it.[23]

～

The root cause of the war in Bosnia, as well as in Croatia, was that it was hard for the Serbs living there to accept the right of self-determination in republics inside Yugoslavia so long as their own right of self-determination within those administrative entities was denied.

However, the basic issue here is not a matter of the details of those tragedies, which can be lengthily discussed, but in the logic of the argument. Of course, nobody can reproach the West for intervening in Rwanda to stop genocide, because no such intervention took place. The problem is that the mainstream discourse uses nonintervention in situations where it might have been justified (although it remains to be seen what would have been the nature and consequences of such an intervention) to prepare public opinion to accept other interventions that do in fact take place but in very different circumstances. The "lessons of history" are always the same: denunciation of our supposed indifference to the suffering of others and encouragement of military intervention. But there are other lessons that could be drawn: for example, that it would have been better not to destabilize the Sihanouk regime in Cambodia, or to encourage Izetbegovic to reject the Lisbon accord: in a word, to intervene less. More than four decades later, President Clinton apologized for U.S. policy toward Guatemala, but neither he nor other U.S. leaders drew the "lesson of history" that the United States would do better not to interfere in the domestic affairs of other states.[24] This asymmetry in official discourse has no basis in fact or logic but simply reflects the desire of governments to overcome their own population's reluctance to engage in foreign adventures.

Risks for the Future

Finally, there are two aspects of "North-South" economic relations that should be mentioned because they are directly linked to problems of domination and potential military conflicts. The first problem concerns our dependence on the Third World.

The expression may sound surprising since we are used to hearing that "we" are helping "them." Moreover, a prominent school of postcolonial commentary has sought to convince us that colonialism played only a minor role in the West's economic development. That argument will be briefly discussed in the following section, but even if it were so, it would be necessary to acknowledge that the situation is constantly evolving in the direction of a growing dependence. For one thing, the traditional role of colonies, which is to provide raw materials, is constantly increasing. Our development model makes Europe and the United States critically dependent on petroleum imports. For another, a growing fraction of manufactured goods come from ex-colonies or former semi-colonies. This problem is usually criticized from the angle of outsourcing and job losses in the developed countries, but can also be seen as a form of dependence: what would we do if those goods were no longer provided or became more expensive? Or if the currency accumulated by the sale of those goods ended up being used to modify the relationship of forces between, say, China and the United States? Of course, it can be said in response that the dependence is mutual: they provide raw materials and unskilled labor, and we provide high technology. But the scientific and technological development of China and India cast serious doubts on that argument.[25]

In addition to all that, there is the brain drain: skimping on education in the rich countries, along with the universalization of entertainment culture, is leading to the progressive destruction of our public school systems. This decline is more advanced in the United States than in Europe, but Europe is making successful efforts to catch up. Nevertheless, our industries, in particular the arms industry, need brains. It is enough to take a tour of American universities, or even of European laboratories, to realize that the education systems of poor countries are increasingly making up for the deficit of schooling in the rich countries.

∼

The Decline of Science and Engineering

"But because of the steady erosion of science, math and engineering, education in U.S. high schools, our cold war generation of American scientists is not being fully replenished. We traditionally filled the gap with Indian, Chinese, and other immigrant brainpower. But post-9/11, many of these foreign engineers are not coming here anymore, and, because the world is now flat and wired, many others can stay home and innovate without having to emigrate."[26]

"According to the New York Times, the U.S. military is paying hundreds of thousands of dollars to send scientists on a screenwriting course in Los Angeles, with the aim of producing movies and television shows that portray scientists in a flattering light. It is being billed as a radical solution to one of America's most vexing long-term national security problems: the drastic decline in the number of U.S. students pursuing science and engineering."[27]

∼

Leaving aside the immoral aspect of this situation, one can wonder just how stable it all is. Isn't the Chinese strategy of accumulating capital more efficient in the long run than the American strategy of gigantic deficits to finance the accumulation of weapons? (After all, the Chinese strategy is more or less similar to what the United States did in the 19th century.) Writing over a century ago, the economist John Hobson, quoted below, was remarkably prescient about the tendency of imperialism, except for an essential aspect: neither China nor India can any longer be exploited at will. The twentieth century, through its wars and revolutions, saw a turn of the tide in the relationship of forces created between the West and the Third World during the previous centuries. Colonialism was replaced by neocolonialism and Europe by the United States, but this system of domination is much weaker than the one that went before. Moreover, it is in trouble everywhere: Asia has in large part gained real independence, that is, it has freed itself from neocolonialism as well as colonialism, with the notable exception of Pakistan, Afghanistan. and certain parts of former Soviet Asia.[28] Latin America seems to be emerging from a long period of dictatorships and political discouragement and turning in the direction of greater independence. Western domination persists in Africa and the Arab world, but for how long? If the Iraqi resistance is not crushed, and for the moment nothing indicates it will be, it could sound the death knell of neocolonialism.

The dominant power of the nineteenth century was England. It lost its status to the United States, without direct conflict between the two, but nevertheless through two world wars against the rising great power of the period, Germany. Will the United States accept peacefully the loss of its status of unique superpower if the development of China or India leaves no choice? That is the question. For now it is clear that all leading U.S. strategists, from Zbigniew Brzezinski to the neoconservatives, are determined to avoid that scenario at all costs, even resorting to the militarization of space, source of incalculable new dangers.[29]

Another problem is simply the exhaustion of natural resources, which is potentially more dangerous than problems of pollution or even of climate change, because the struggle for dwindling resources is very likely to be a factor in future wars. The West absorbs a disproportionate share of the planet's natural resources, though at the same time promoting its way of life as an example for others to follow. Of course, one can always hope that technological innovation, for example, mastery of nuclear fusion, a spectacular improvement in harnessing solar energy, or some other radical breakthrough will provide a miracle solution to such problems. But it is unreasonable in the present state of our knowledge to behave as if such a solution is sure to emerge. Nature is under no obligation to be kind to us and to satisfy our every whim. We are in the position of those who climb a ladder and then, having safely reached the top, tell others to follow while pulling the ladder up with us. There is something fairly comical about the dismay aroused in our countries by the increase in China's energy needs, an increase that is the inevitable consequence of the path of development we ourselves are so proud of having pioneered.

If we start to think about all the direct and indirect effects of our domination strategies and the violence they provoke, the West can no longer be seen primarily as the guardian of admirable universal values, which it puts into practice better than the rest of the world, but also as a considerable source of suffering and oppression.

~

Silent Genocide

The sanctions imposed on Iraq from 1990 to 2003, combined with the devastating effects of the 1991 Gulf War which targeted civilian infrastructures in particular, had catastrophic effects for the civilian population. Hundreds of thousands of children died because of those sanctions. The United Nations coordinator for humanitarian aid to Iraq, Dennis Halliday, resigned in September 1998, declaring: "We are in the process of destroying an entire society. It is as simple and terrifying as that. It is illegal and immoral." When told that the effects of the sanctions were due to the indifference of the regime to its own population, Halliday replied: "That's absolute garbage, the fact is that before Saddam Hussein got himself into trouble in Iran, and then of course in Kuwait, they had invested massively in civilian infrastructure. Health care clinics, rural clinics, education, 10,000 schools scattered throughout the country, an educational and health care system which was the envy of all its Arab neighbors. Iraq had a very widespread food distribution system of its own before we got involved."[30]

Halliday's successor, Hans von Sponeck, resigned in February 2000 for the same reasons, and Jutta Burghardt, who directed the World Food Program for Iraq, followed suit shortly thereafter. In a devastating report on the sanctions policy, Marc Bossuyt wrote:

> The sanctions regime against Iraq has as its clear purpose the deliberate infliction on the Iraqi people of conditions of life (lack of adequate food, medicines, etc.) calculated to bring about its physical destruction in whole or in part. It does not matter that this deliberate physical destruction has as its ostensible objective the security of the region. Once clear evidence was available that thousands of civilians were dying and that hundreds of thousands would die in the future as the Security Council continued the sanctions, the deaths were no longer an unintended side effect—the Security Council was responsible for all known consequences of its actions. The sanctioning bodies cannot be absolved from having the "intent to destroy" the Iraqi people. The United States Ambassador to the United Nations [Madeleine Albright] in fact admitted this; when questioned whether the half-million deaths were "worth it," she replied: "We think the price is worth it." The States imposing the sanctions could raise questions under the genocide Convention.[31]

~

Moreover, although it may not be entirely rational, one cannot help feeling a particular revulsion at the sight of the strong attacking the weak: the Israelis installing checkpoints and colonies in the occupied territories, or the United States bombing all of Indochina, relentlessly destroying the Sandinista revolution, depriving Cuba of anything that could help it achieve its public health goals, and condemning hundreds of thousands of Iraqis to slow death. Seen from a distance of space or time, the West presents an image of widespread indifference to criminal policies pursued with a perfectly clear conscience, symbolized by the "humanitarian" interventionist Bernard Kouchner providing moralistic cover for the cynicism of a Donald Rumsfeld.

~

Hobson on the Future of Imperialism in 1902

The greater part of Western Europe might then assume the appearance and character already exhibited by tracts of country in the South of England, in the Riviera and in the tourist-ridden or residential parts of Italy and Switzerland, little clusters of wealthy aristocrats drawing dividends and pensions from the Far East, with a somewhat larger group of professional retainers and tradesmen and a larger body of personal servants and workers in the transport trade and in the final stages of production of the more perishable goods; all the main arterial industries would have disappeared, the staple foods and manufactures flowing in as tribute from Asia and Africa. … We have foreshadowed the possibility of even a larger alliance of Western states, a European federation of great powers which, so far from forwarding the cause of world civilization, might introduce the gigantic peril of a Western parasitism, a group of advanced industrial nations, whose upper classes drew vast tribute from Asia and Africa, with which they supported great tame masses of retainers, no longer engaged in the staple industries of agriculture and manufacture, but kept in the performance of personal or minor industrial services under the control of a new financial

aristocracy. Let those who would scout such a theory (it would be better
to say: prospect) as undeserving of consideration examine the economic
and social condition of districts in Southern England today which are
already reduced to this condition, and reflect upon the vast extension of
such a system which might be rendered feasible by the subjection of China
to the economic control of similar groups of financiers, investors, and political and business officials, draining the greatest potential reservoir of profit
the world has ever known, in order to consume it in Europe. The situation
is far too complex, the play of world forces far too incalculable, to render
this or any other single interpretation of the future very probable; but the
influences which govern the imperialism of Western Europe today are
moving in this direction, and, unless counteracted or diverted, make
towards some such consummation.[32]

~

The Lesson of Guatemala

On June 17, 1952, the Guatemalan congress adopted an agrarian reform
law introduced by the country's popular president, Jacobo Arbenz, elected in 1950.[33] The law was hailed as a "constructive and democratic"
model by the U.N. Food and Agriculture Organization. Uncultivated land
on large holdings was expropriated (with compensation) and distributed
to landless peasants, descendants of the Mayans who had been crushed by
the Spanish conquest. To give the new small property owners the means
to make good use of their land, a system of low-interest farm credit was
instituted. Literacy courses were introduced into the countryside. Finally,
the government sponsored a road-building program to break the foreign
monopoly on transport and enable small farmers to market their produce.
Far from collectivizing land in the Soviet manner, the reform favored small,
private family farms. It aimed at creating the conditions for a modern capitalist economy.

Two years after introducing his agrarian reform, Jacobo Arbenz was driven out of office on June 27, 1954, by a military putsch organized by the CIA. The CIA at the time was headed by Allen Dulles, brother of John Foster Dulles, President Eisenhower's secretary of state. Both Dulles brothers had professional links with the United Fruit Company, which owned vast plantations in the country. Even though Arbenz's reforms did not directly threaten United Fruit, the bad example was unwelcome.

A "liberation" force was armed in neighboring Honduras. Despite their respect for Arbenz, his own officers backed off from confrontation with the North American superpower. Abandoned by his army, Arbenz resigned, hoping that this sacrifice would ease the pressure and save his reforms. The United States claimed to be opposed only to the "red" president who "threatened democracy" in the hemisphere, and not to the reforms. But without Arbenz, the country was turned over to unprincipled and incompetent officers who canceled the reforms and plunged Guatemala into decades of bloody dictatorship and poverty, marked by massacres of tens of thousands of peasants. The Guatemalan tragedy is an exemplary illustration of the real existing "defense of democracy" as it has been practiced by the United States. It is characterized by:

- A paranoid attitude on the part of the superpower toward the slightest challenge.

- Demonization of adversaries. In those days, it was enough to call the victim a "communist." Later, the label became "terrorist." In any case, demonization prevents their side of the story from being taken into consideration.

- Arrogant ignorance. What Washington thinks it knows about foreign countries tends to come either from big companies with interests there (such as United Fruit) or reactionary lobbies linked to them, including rich locals eager to use U.S. power to protect their unjust privileges. The more skeptical views of a few relatively lucid diplomats or intelligence analysts almost never reach the desks of top decision makers.

- Media conformism. U.S. media relay the official U.S. government version of events without serious investigation. Opposing views are dismissed as absurd.

- The "bipartisan" unanimity of the ruling political class. The Democratic president Truman had begun plans for the Guatemala putsch, carried out under the Republican Eisenhower.

- Total disregard for international law, coupled with threats toward whoever wants to apply it to the United States. In June 1954, when France wanted to support Guatemala's urgent appeal to the U.N. Security Council to stop the armed aggression mounted by the United States in neighboring Honduras and Nicaragua, U.S. diplomats reacted with rage. In response to threats from Washington, both France and Britain finally abstained. Dag Hammarskjöld, who was U.N. secretary general at the time, called this U.S. blockage of the Guatemala problem "the hardest blow so far" against the United Nations. Many more such blows were to follow.

- The crushing of the most democratic or progressive forces in a given country on the pretext of favoring a supposed "third force," more democratic in a Western sense, but which does not in fact exist.

It must be admitted that hypocrisy and fanaticism can very well coexist. What may seem odd is that America's particular fanaticism is on behalf of "moderation"—a moderation of the rich and privileged who want to hang on to what they've got. In reality, the dynamics of American imperialism lead to upheaval and transformation, not in the sense of spreading the "American dream" around the world, as claimed, but toward unforeseen and tragic chaos.

3

Questions to Human Rights Defenders

The ideas criticized in this book are often implicit, but have recently been more explicitly expressed by groups defining themselves as liberals, democrats, and progressives. A perfect illustration of these ideas is to be found in a 2005 book, entitled *A Matter of Principle: Humanitarian Arguments for War in Iraq*, a collective work by a number of writers who argue in favor of the war in Iraq on the basis of human rights.[1] The authors consider that the United States had not only the right but the duty to use its superior military force to intervene and liberate the Iraqi people from the dictatorship of Saddam Hussein. Neither the absence of weapons of mass destruction in Iraq nor the fact that such an intervention flouts international law troubles them in the least, convinced as they are that human rights are a value far more fundamental than respect for international law. Many of them situate themselves in the center or on the left of the political spectrum, and part of their argument consists in denouncing the rest of the left for hesitating to come out firmly on the side of humanitarian war. They associate such hesitations with the left's insufficient hostility toward the Soviet Union during the Cold War, as well as with the failure of Western countries to have waged a preventive war against Hitler.

The same arguments are to be found in a statement titled "The Euston Manifesto," issued in the spring of 2006 by a group of British Laborites and signed by a number of Americans, including Marc Cooper of *The Nation* and Michael Walzer of the Institute for Advanced Study (Princeton), co-editor of *Dissent*. Their "statement of principles" provides several potential arguments for war: human rights for all, opposing anti-Americanism, a new internationalism. Characteristically, the "errors of the past" are cited to discredit rejection of wars waged by democratic countries, and the lies that led up to the invasion of Iraq are dismissed as no longer relevant.

~

Excerpts from "The Euston Manifesto"

Drawing the lesson of the disastrous history of left apologetics over the crimes of Stalinism and Maoism, as well as more recent exercises in the same vein (some of the reaction to the crimes of 9/11, the excuse-making for suicide-terrorism, the disgraceful alliances lately set up inside the "anti-war" movement with illiberal theocrats), we reject the notion that there are no opponents on the left. We reject, similarly, the idea that there can be no opening to ideas and individuals to our right. Leftists who make common cause with, or excuses for, antidemocratic forces should be criticized in clear and forthright terms. ...

The founding supporters of this statement took different views on the military intervention in Iraq, both for and against. We recognize that it was possible reasonably to disagree about the justification for the intervention, the manner in which it was carried through, the planning (or lack of it) for the aftermath, and the prospects for the successful implementation of democratic change. We are, however, united in our view about the reactionary, semi-fascist and murderous character of the Ba'athist regime in Iraq, and we recognize its overthrow as a liberation of the Iraqi people. We are also united in the view that, since the day on which this occurred, the proper concern of genuine liberals and members of the Left should have been the battle to put in place in Iraq a democratic political order and to rebuild the country's infrastructure, to create after decades of the most brutal oppression a life for Iraqis which those living in democratic countries take for granted—rather than picking through the rubble of the arguments over intervention.[2]

≈

In short, errors of the distant past (support for the alleged "motherland of socialism") must be the source of endless shame and disgrace, whereas quite recent errors—or rather, lies—are not worth mentioning. This forgetfulness conveniently obscures the origins of the war in a policy designed to overthrow the Iraqi regime, not for the welfare of the Iraqi people, but for what a particular group of neoconservative policymakers, calling themselves the Project for a New American Century, described as "our vital interests."

∼

The Origins of the Invasion of Iraq:
Excerpt from a Letter Sent to President Clinton

The only acceptable strategy is one that eliminates the possibility that Iraq will be able to use or threaten to use weapons of mass destruction. In the near term, this means a willingness to undertake military action as diplomacy is clearly failing. In the long term, it means removing Saddam Hussein and his regime from power. That now needs to become the aim of American foreign policy. We urge you to articulate this aim, and to turn your Administration's attention to implementing a strategy for removing Saddam's regime from power. This will require a full complement of diplomatic, political and military efforts. Although we are fully aware of the dangers and difficulties in implementing this policy, we believe the dangers of failing to do so are far greater. We believe the U.S. has the authority under existing UN resolutions to take the necessary steps, including military steps, to protect our vital interests in the Gulf. In any case, American

policy cannot continue to be crippled by a misguided insistence on unanimity in the UN Security Council. [3]

∿

In France, where few people took the WMD threat seriously, the main
argument in favor of the war in Iraq—voiced notably by Bernard
Kouchner—was humanitarian intervention. And by now, what conceivable
argument other than the defense of human rights and democracy could
possibly justify that war, as well as the ongoing occupation and bloodshed?
Once it is recognized that the invasion was illegal and the pretexts false,
why not simply demand that the Americans get out? And yet no Western
government and practically no political movement has drawn that conclusion. Why? Because, we are told, it is now necessary to "stabilize" Iraq, to
"construct democracy" there, etc. As a result, even if it is true that many
organizations and intellectuals who defend human rights were initially
opposed to the war, they have found themselves more or less obliged to
support the ongoing war of occupation until the situation is "stabilized."

Such reasoning is the culmination of an ideological process that began
thirty years ago. At the end of the war in Vietnam, and following Nixon's
disgrace, the prestige of the United States had sunk to a new low. President
Carter, whose political innocence was in sharp contrast to the open cynicism of the Kissinger-Nixon tandem, was able to present human rights as
"the soul of American foreign policy."[4] This was a somewhat innovative
approach, since up till then the principal objective proclaimed by the
United States was to build strong states with staunchly anticommunist
governments in the Third World, with scant regard for human rights. It
was that "nation-building" policy that had led the United States to support or install various governments in South Vietnam, with disastrous
results. Moralizing rhetoric combined with perfectly cynical practice
(notably in Afghanistan) was amazingly successful. In Europe, especially
in France, where revolutionary illusions were fading, the intelligentsia

took charge of a major reversal, from the systematic criticism of power, associated with Sartre and Foucault, to its systematic defense—especially the power of the United States—symbolized by the emergence of the "new philosophers" as media stars. Defense of human rights became the theme and principal argument of the new political offensive against both the socialist bloc and Third World countries emerging from colonialism.

~

The Origins of Soviet Intervention in Afghanistan

Zbigniew Brzezinski: According to the official version of history, CIA aid to the mujahiddin began during 1980, that is, after the Soviet army had invaded Afghanistan on December 24, 1979. But the truth, kept secret up to now, is quite different: it was in fact on July 3, 1979, that President Carter signed the first directive on clandestine aid to opponents of the pro-Soviet regime in Kabul. And on that very day I wrote a note to the president in which I explained to him that in my view aid was going to bring about a Soviet military intervention.

Nouvel Observateur. When the Soviets justified their intervention by claiming that they meant to counter a secret intervention by the United States in Afghanistan, no one believed them. However, there was some truth in that. ... You don't regret anything today?

Brzezinski: Regret what? That secret operation was an excellent idea. Its effect was to draw the Russians into the Afghan trap and you want me to regret it? The day the Soviets officially crossed the border, I wrote to President Carter roughly the following: "We now have the opportunity to give the USSR its own Vietnam War."[5]

~

The basic idea of this school of thought is simple enough: since democracy and human rights are much more respected in the West than elsewhere, it is our right and even our duty to do whatever we can to see to it that these rights are extended to the rest of humanity. Moreover, that obligation takes priority, since human rights come first; they are even the precondition for development.

The success of that ideology in transforming the Western left has been quite remarkable. Human rights, whose invocation in the 1970s was a way for the United States to restore its reputation after the Vietnamese debacle, were taken up by many progressive movements as their primary, if not sole, objective. Worse still, numerous left intellectuals consider it their mission to criticize Western governments for their excessive caution and timidity. To hear their complaints, one might gather that the main problem in the world today is the failure of the West to intervene in enough places (Chechnya, Tibet, Kurdistan, Sudan) and with enough force to promote and export its genuine values, democracy and human rights.

In the moderate version of this ideology, we are only called upon to protest, by demonstrations or letter writing, against human rights violations committed in other places. The tougher versions demand economic and diplomatic sanctions or even, if necessary, that the West have recourse to military intervention.

The main thing wrong with the "tough" version, the one calling for military intervention, stems from the ambiguity of the "we" in statements such as "We should intervene in order to … " The "we" does not usually refer to a particular group to which the person making such recommendations belongs, as would have been the case, for example, with the volunteers who joined the International Brigades during the Spanish Civil War, but to armed forces powerful enough to intervene effectively, in particular those of the United States. During the conflicts in Bosnia and Kosovo, a certain number of Western intellectuals fancied themselves following in the Spanish footsteps of Malraux, Orwell, and Hemingway. But, unlike their predecessors, they largely remained safely at home or ensconced in the same hotel, rather than entering the fray, while the International Brigades and the Spanish Republican Army were replaced by the U.S. Air Force.

Now, nothing in United States policy indicates the slightest sincere concern for human rights and democracy. Assigning it the prime task of defending these values is strange indeed. Moreover, to call on an *army* to wage a *war* for *human rights* implies a naive vision of what armies are and do, as well as a magical belief in the myth of short, clean, "surgical" wars. The example of Iraq shows that it is possible to know when a war starts but not when it will end, and it is totally utopian to expect an army that is under constant attack from guerrilla forces not to have recourse to torture in order to obtain information. The French used it massively in Algeria. The Americans used it in Vietnam and again in Iraq. Yet both the French and American torturers were citizens of "democratic countries, respectful of human rights" —yes, but when they were at home, and in periods of relative social peace.

∽

Kouchner and Truth

Dialogue between Bernard Kouchner and Alija Izetbegovic, in the presence of Richard Holbrooke. Kouchner speaks first:

—You remember President Mitterrand's visit?

—Let me thank you once again.

—In the course of that conversation you spoke of the existence of "extermination camps" in Bosnia. You repeated that in front of the journalists. That provoked considerable emotion throughout the world. François sent me to Omarska and we opened other prisons. They were horrible places, but people were not systematically exterminated. Did you know that?

—Yes. I thought that my revelations could precipitate bombings. I saw the reaction of the French and the others—I was mistaken.

—You understood at Helsinki that President Bush senior would not react, Holbrooke added.

—Yes, I tried, but the assertion was false. There were no extermination camps whatever the horror of those places.

Kouchner concludes:

—The conversation was magnificent, that man at death's door hid nothing
from us of his historic role. Richard and I expressed our immense admiration.[6]

∽

It is indeed a fairly remarkable indirect effect of the human rights ideology that torture in Iraq is almost universally denounced, but not the occupation. Yet torture is the result of occupation. This came to be understood in
the case of the French war in Algiers, when revelations of torture by the
French military stimulated calls to end the conflict. An army that finds itself
the target for resistance fighters who are like fish in the sea is inexorably led
to try to gain information by force. If one calls for military intervention, one
is calling for war and occupation, and in that case, in effect calling for torture.

Well-meaning people can claim that torture doesn't work, but unfortunately, that is far from true. Torture unquestionably enabled the French to
dismantle the Front for National Liberation in Algiers, even if it did not
make it possible to maintain French control of Algeria. Nor should we forget that many insurrections end up being crushed—for example, all those
in Latin America after the Cuban revolution—and that torture often played
a major role in their defeat.

In Washington, alarmists liken Iraq to Vietnam, while some in the
administration may more optimistically be thinking of El Salvador.[7] But no
serious person can see bright prospects for human rights.

∽

The Monoply of Violence

In the war against the militias, every door American troops crash
through, every civilian bystander shot—there will be many—will make matters worse, for a while. Nevertheless, the first task of the occupation
remains the first task of government: to establish a monopoly on violence.

—George Will[8]

∽

Another thing basically wrong with the tough version of human rights ideology is the failure to recognize that just because a society is democratic in its internal political life does not in any way imply that it will have a generous attitude toward the rest of the world. To take an extreme contemporary example, Israel is without any doubt the most democratic country in its region in regard to its own population, or at any rate the Jewish part of that population. But the least one can say is that the state of Israel cannot be relied on to protect the rights of the Palestinians in the occupied territories, or those of the Lebanese. And the same could be said for the populations of the colonial empires. Their European masters were already "democracies respectful of human rights," who used the "defense of human rights" to legitimize their colonial enterprise. British liberal imperialists discovered in the late nineteenth century that presenting foreign interventions as moral crusades was particularly effective in whipping up popular support in a parliamentary democracy with a press eager to denounce foreign villainy. King Leopold II of Belgium justified his conquest of the Congo by the fight against Arab slave dealers. His own treatment of the native Congolese scarcely stands as a monument to human rights.

The fact that the United States is a democratic country with a free press doesn't change much, or in any case less than is claimed, for the victims of U.S. sanctions and bombings. Indeed, the "free" press is remarkably uniform when it comes to foreign policy, and being free makes it a more efficient propaganda tool. Citizens of countries where the press is censored by the government tend to catch on and end up not believing anything it says. The U.S. press finally got around to criticizing the war in Vietnam, but only after many years and countless dead and, above all, only after the 1968 Vietnamese Tet offensive convinced American elites that the war was costing too much, both in military losses and domestic disorder. But no similar protest could be heard in regard to the genocidal embargo imposed on the Iraqi people in the 1990s.[9] And as for the 2003 war, all the official lies were diligently echoed by the mainstream media. Once again, it was only when a strong Iraqi resistance made itself felt that U.S. media showed signs of having second thoughts.

The Lancet Study

In November 2004, the prestigious British medical review *The Lancet* published the results of a study of excess mortality caused by the invasion of Iraq. Dr. Les Roberts, who led the study, concluded: "Making conservative assumptions we think that about 100,000 excess deaths, or more, have happened since the 2003 invasion of Iraq. Violence accounted for most of the excess deaths and air strikes from coalition forces accounted for most of the violent deaths."[10] One of the conservative postulates of the study was not to take into consideration data concerning Fallujah. The study was ignored or discredited in the United States and to a lesser extent in Britain. Media did not hesitate to echo a comment made by a Human Rights Watch military expert, Marc E. Garlasco, to the effect that the figures seemed exaggerated, even though Garlasco admitted that he had not read the *Lancet* study when he made that comment.

Dr. Roberts has used the same methods to study the conflict in Eastern Congo, arriving at an estimate of 1,700,000 deaths, a figure that failed to arouse skepticism among Western media or politicians. On the contrary, both Tony Blair and Colin Powell cited its conclusions. As Dr. Roberts remarked, "It is odd that the logic of epidemiology embraced by the press every day regarding new drugs or health risks somehow changes when the mechanism of death is their armed forces."[11]

The basic objection to the idea of using the U.S. Army for humanitarian purposes can be summed up in a few words: the purpose of an army, in the best of cases, is to defend its own country, or else to attack others. Neither of these aims, even if the first can be considered legitimate, is altruistic.

Everything about an army, its equipment, its training, and above all its mindset (esprit de corps and patriotism), are designed to serve those aims. So why hope that an army can be used for supposedly altruistic purposes?

Still, the partisans of humanitarian intervention stress that the purpose of "modern" armies is no longer simply to defend their own country but to help others and save oppressed populations. This implies waging a war without too many casualties on the side of the "liberator." Otherwise, the soldiers' families will ask what their children are dying for. This is what happened during the summer of 2005, when the mother of a soldier killed in Iraq, Cindy Sheehan, camped outside the Crawford, Texas, ranch where Bush was spending his vacation. She wanted to ask him face-to-face the question "What is the noble cause my son died for?"[12] For the partisans of the war who attacked her action, she had a simple response: "The army is recruiting and lacks personnel. Why don't *you* join up?" Now that the army recruits women as well as men, and recalls reservists over the age of forty, it is not so easy to evade such a question. It can be addressed to all the partisans of humanitarian wars once these wars are not short and sweet.

What shows that the problem raised above is at least implicitly recognized by the war apologists is that they employ a double discourse. For the intellectuals and the elite, it is all about the right to intervene, humanitarian interventions, etc. For the rest of the population, it is all about the "war against terror," weapons of mass destruction—that is, about threats and dangers from which we must defend ourselves. The majority of the population have enough good sense to understand that if the idea is to accomplish altruistic deeds there are a whole lot of things to do besides waging war. On the other hand, they may be ready to make sacrifices for self-defense. Unfortunately, they often lack the means of obtaining information other than from television. Intellectuals, on the other hand, have the means to be better informed and are often aware that the threats brandished by governments are exaggerated. Thus they are the ones who invent and interiorize the ideology of humanitarian war as a legitimization mechanism.

Marx spoke of religion as the opium of the people; the French liberal philosopher Raymond Aron ironically called Marxism "the opium of the intellectuals." Whether or not that was the case in his day, one can say that today that opium has become the ideology of humanitarian intervention.

The moderate versions of the human rights ideology, those which do not necessarily advocate war but encourage intervention in one form or another in various Third World countries, or steady denunciation of whatever is going on there, should also be subjected to criticism. This is because, by harping on certain aspects and overlooking others, they create a distorted vision of the world that enables the tough version of human rights ideology to prosper and marginalizes opposition to imperial wars.

Even admitting that human rights are both highly desirable and far more respected in "our" countries than elsewhere, three fundamental conceptual problems remain. The first is the problem of transition. How can a society pass from a feudal or colonial situation, in which the very idea of human rights is not formulated, to a situation comparable to what we know in our societies today? And do we have something to teach the rest of the world in this matter? The second problem stems from the inclusion in the U.N.'s 1948 Declaration of two types of rights: individual and political rights on the one hand, and economic and social rights on the other. To what extent are these rights compatible with each other, and if they are not, are there priorities between them? The third problem concerns the effects and the moral value of the ritual denunciations of human rights violations in poor countries by various organizations in the rich countries.

∼

Free Media

Shortly after Hurricane Katrina devastated New Orleans, the African-American singer Kanye West stated during a live broadcast devoted to raising funds for the victims: "I hate the way they portray us in the media. You see a black family, it says, 'They're looting.' You see a white family, it says, 'They're looking for food.' And, you know, it's been five days [waiting for federal help] because most of the people are black. ... George Bush doesn't care about black people!"

What is even more revealing is the reaction of the television network, NBC, to these remarks: "Tonight's telecast was a live television event wrought with emotion. Kanye West departed from the scripted comments that were prepared for him, and his opinions in no way represent the views of the networks." West's comments were edited out of the West Coast broadcast. Now, what was it we criticized Soviet media for?[13]

∽

The Question of Transition and Development

Just imagine a mafia godfather who, as he grows old, decides to defend law and order and starts attacking his lesser colleagues in crime, preaching brotherly love and the sanctity of human life—all this while holding on to his ill-gotten gains and the income they provide. Who would fail to denounce such flagrant hypocrisy? And yet, strangely enough, scarcely anyone seems to see the parallel with the West's self-anointed role as defender of human rights, although the similarities are considerable.

Let's start by asking ourselves what the historical process was by which we managed to reach the present high level of civilization in which we take such pride. Certainly it was not only democracy, the free market, or respect for human rights that got us here. We cannot even claim to owe our success solely to Christian charity or to the philosophers of the Enlightenment. Wars, colonialism, child labor, autocracy, and pillage are also very much part of the roots of our present civilization. It cannot reasonably be denied that the actions of Bismarck, Queen Victoria, both Napoleons, Leopold II, and Theodore Roosevelt, not to mention the conquistadores and the slave traders, also contributed to our development. What is certain is that their behavior was far from being altogether compatible with human rights.

Of course, it will be said that human rights are a universal value and that nothing—no special economic or cultural circumstances—can justify violating them. But here's the rub. To start with, our mafioso would not be wrong, in the abstract, to defend respect for the law and brotherly love. But he would be hypocritical. The same reproach can be addressed to the Western discourse on human rights and for exactly the same reasons. Once it is acknowledged that human rights only became respectable in our countries (at least in regard to our domestic affairs) after a long historical process, and in particular after a long cultural, social, and economic development, we must ask ourselves how countries that find themselves at another level of socioeconomic development can attain the one we enjoy; and above all how they can do so while adhering to the human rights standards that our own societies did not respect in the least when we were at the stage of development where they are now.

Again, it will be said that respect for human rights and development are not opposed to each other, and that they are even complementary. Unfortunately, things are not so simple. It is easy to point to several examples of factors that unquestionably contributed to our own development, but from which Third World countries cannot benefit today. These factors create an asymmetry between our past and their present situation, as well as contradicting human rights as we understand them.

The first and most important of these factors is obviously colonialism. What was the impact of colonialism either on the development of the West or on the underdevelopment of non-European societies? This is a matter of considerable dispute, and there seems to be no recognized way to measure this impact with any precision. But that is just the problem: nobody really knows what enables a society to develop economically. In particular, what is the role of cultural factors? For example, how can one measure the impact on our development of the racist sense of superiority that flourished in the colonial era, and which gave Europeans their overriding self-confidence? Is it more or less important than the Protestant spirit emphasized by Max

Weber? These questions are not so easy to answer, and raising them only gives a hint of the multitude of difficulties involved.

To get an idea of the difficulty of measuring the impact of colonialism, let us try to imagine a world similar to ours but where Europe is the only continent on the planet to have emerged from the oceans. In that world, there would be no slave trade, no America, no colonial expansion, no cheap immigrant labor, no Middle Eastern petroleum, no Siberian gas. Who can say what our society would be like? And if there is no answer to that question, what sense does it make to say that colonialism has had little impact on our development?

Another of these factors is the issue of immigration and emigration. Back in the days when Europeans "had too many children" it was easy to send them off to populate the rest of the world. Some even saw this as a way to avoid social unrest and revolutions, whose repression would obviously have entailed "human rights violations" comparable to those observed in numerous poor countries today. But when the population explosion in the Third World provokes crises, where can they export their excess population? To our countries, of course, but only to do whatever hard labor is needed at the bottom of the social scale. This is a far cry from the situation of white Europeans who set themselves up in Rhodesia by expropriating as much land as they could ride around in a day on horseback.

~

Empire and Civil War

The journalist William Thomas Stead recounts that his close friend Cecil Rhodes told him in 1895, in regard to his imperialist ideas: "I was in the East End of London (a working-class quarter) yesterday and attended a meeting of the unemployed. I listened to the wild speeches, which were just a cry for 'bread! bread!' and on my way home I pondered over the scene and I became more than ever convinced of the importance of imperialism. ... My cherished idea is a solution for the social problem, i.e.,

in order to save the 40,000,000 inhabitants of the United Kingdom from
a bloody civil war, we colonial statesmen must acquire new lands to settle
the surplus population, to provide new markets for the goods produced
in the factories and mines. The Empire, as I have always said, is a bread
and butter question. If you want to avoid civil war, you must become
imperialists."[14]

~

To come back to the present, the right to leave one's country to flee
persecution (guaranteed by Article 14 of the U.N. Declaration) is applied
in an extraordinarily selective manner by the United States. For example,
out of more than 24,000 Haitians intercepted by Coast Guard forces on
their way to U.S. shores between 1981 and 1990, only eleven were granted the right of asylum, compared to 75,000 Cubans in the same situation.
For Cubans, asylum is automatic.[15] It takes a heavy dose of preconceived
ideas to consider that all the former were "economic" and all the latter
"political" refugees. Or consider Article 13 of the Declaration, which
ensures the right to leave one's own country. During the final stages of the
Cold War, the United States was unflinching in its demand that Soviet
Jews be allowed to leave their country, mainly to emigrate to Israel (an
emigration that ran into Soviet objections concerning the cost to the state
of having educated the candidates for emigration). But the same Article
13 also guarantees the right of return to your country of origin. The day
after ratification of the Declaration, the United Nations adopted
Resolution 194, which gave Palestinians driven from their territories the
right to return home (or else to receive compensation). Everyone knows
perfectly well that this return will never take place without a profound
shake-up in the world relationship of forces. On the other hand, the
Israeli settlers who were obliged to leave the Gaza strip colonies they had
illegally occupied received an average of a quarter of a million dollars per
family in compensation.[16]

~

Harvard Law Professor Offers a Solution to Terrorism

Israel should announce an immediate unilateral cessation in retaliation against terrorist attacks. This moratorium would be in effect for a short period, say four or five days, to give the Palestinian leadership an opportunity to respond to the new policy. It would also make it clear to the world that Israel is taking an important step in ending what has become a cycle of violence. Following the end of the moratorium, Israel would institute the following new policy if Palestinian terrorism were to resume. It will announce precisely what it will do in response to the next act of terrorism. For example, it could announce the first act of terrorism following the moratorium will result in the destruction of a small village which has been used as a base for terrorist operations. The residents would be given 24 hours to leave, and then troops will come in and bulldoze all of the buildings. The response will be automatic. The order will have been given in advance of the terrorist attacks and there will be no discretion. The point is to make the automatic destruction of the village the fault of the Palestinian terrorists who had advance warnings of the specific consequences of their action. The soldiers would simply be acting as the means for carrying out a previously announced policy of retaliation against a designated target.

—Alan M. Dershowitz[17]

~

In the last analysis, the cruelest truth in regard to the grand Western declaration about the "free circulation of persons" is illustrated by an anecdote. On a visit to the United States in the 1970s, the Chinese leader Deng Xiao Ping, in response to President Carter's demand that China allow its people to leave, is said to have replied: "Certainly—and how many million Chinese do you want?"

Another factor of contrast between the developed and developing countries is the construction of powerful and stable states. Even the United

States, today the champion of freeing the economy from state interference, built its economic strength thanks to a huge amount of government support: protection of budding industries, favors to railroads and other infrastructure, control of the currency, and public education.[18] And the so-called defense budget of the United States, which amounts today to roughly half of the entire world's military expenditures, that is, more than the rest of the world put together, is at least in part a form of military Keynesianism that allows massive subsidies of high-technology industries.[19]

~

Micheal Ignatieff on Nation-Building

Let's remember just what any free nation can do, provided its resources and international law permit. It can, for instance, develop weapons of mass destruction, including nuclear weapons. They can opt out of non-proliferation agreements, especially if an imperial occupation authority forced them to sign. And a free country can develop any other sort of weapon you can think of; for example, advanced antitank and antiaircraft missiles. It can buy and sell such weapons, to our enemies, just as we buy and sell them to the enemies of other countries. It can raise large armed forces. It can develop electronic warfare capabilities. It can form alliances. Maybe a free democratic Iraq would ally itself with Iran, Pakistan, North Korea, a newly radicalized Turkey, perhaps China as well. The rights of these free nations would certainly include launching spy satellites which orbited over the U.S., and acquiring long-range nuclear missiles. So a free country, a really free country, can not only cease to service our lust for raw materials. It can also get together with other countries, with the express objective of challenging our supremacy.

In other words, what is so unutterably silly about [Michael] Ignatieff's proposal is the idea that genuine self-determination or "freedom" could ever be the objective of an imperial power. Building a free nation, if possible, is dangerous: why not take on the much easier task of building an enslaved client state? Ignatieff claims that imperialism's opposition to "modern nationalism" is a mistake. It is not. Imperial powers fight modern nationalism because it threatens them, and because it can and quite often is defeated. Vietnam was an exceptional case because it had strong Russian and important Chinese support. When that kind of support is lacking, the interest of all imperialisms—and even Ignatieff admits that imperial powers pursue their own interests—is to prevent rather than to foster nation-building. This is why, for better or more often for worse, imperialism has always attacked the real nation-builders, men like Abd-el-Krim in Morocco, Joshua Nkomo, Castro, Lumumba, Gandhi, Bose, Ben Bella and other Algerian revolutionaries, Janio Quadros of Brazil, Nasser, Sukarno in Indonesia, Arbenz of Guatemala, Mossadegh and Khomeini of Iran, Mao and Zhou Enlai. All imperialisms must oppose the building of free nations as opposed to tame, subject "democracies" like our staunch allies, the Marshall Islands. So real nation-building, even where it is possible, is nothing America would ever want to sponsor.

—Michael Neumann[20]

There was nothing idyllic about the way the strong Western nation-states were built: foreign wars, extermination of indigenous populations, merciless persecution of centrifugal forces within— persecutions that often lasted for several centuries. If the Russians had done with the Chechens what the white Americans did with the Amerindians, there would be no conflict in Chechnya today (of course, I am not recommending such a way of dealing with the problem, but simply suggesting that Westerners show a bit more modesty when they speak of that conflict). If Yugoslavia or China had enjoyed a long period of modern economic development allowing them to reach a dominant position on the world scale, the situation of Kosovo or Tibet might well be similar to that of Brittany or Wales, or, at the worst, Corsica or the Basque country.

The flow of money is another factor. Our foreign aid budgets amount to a tiny fraction of our GNP. And even less if we subtract the share that goes to military cooperation or promotion of our own business interests. For many Third World countries, such aid is a drop in the bucket compared to the usurious interest payments, euphemistically called "debt service," that keep them permanently strapped. Moreover, in many countries, for example Argentina or Indonesia, the debt was largely incurred by former dictatorial regimes that came to power with the support of the creditor powers, notably the United States, the debt being part of the support deal. It's rather as if Mr. X demanded interest payments from Mr. Y for a debt contracted by Mr. Z, who is in fact an accomplice of Mr. X.

It is true that this factor has more to do with the poor countries' possibility of respecting their obligations concerning economic and social rights rather than strictly political rights. But the two are related, as we shall discuss further on. How indeed is it possible to preserve the minimum stability required to establish political rights when a state is ruined, which leads to uprisings—often encouraged from outside? The Yugoslav tragedy illustrates this type of situation, even if, in that case, the economic aspect of the problem was almost completely ignored in favor of analyses stigmatizing "nationalism," principally that of the Serbs, who happened to be the only national group without a sponsoring godfather among the Western powers—unlike the Croats, backed by Germany, or the Bosnian Muslims, whose cause was taken up by the United States.[21]

If you really stop to think about all these aspects of the modern economic development of various countries, you cannot help but be struck by the quantity of suffering involved, and that the first countries to undertake that adventure have had the means to prevent those who came later from *really* following the same course. The first major industrialization, that of Britain, was linked to the conquest of a vast empire providing raw materials, markets, and space for its own population expansion. All the major European powers proceeded to carve out colonies as they industrialized, causing untold suffering to the conquered peoples.[22] In the second great wave of industrialization, the United States, Germany, and Japan all practiced protectionism to build the strength of their industries. The United States had the further advantage of enormous territorial expansion, at the expense of the indigenous population, followed by a Monroe Doctrine "closed door" policy in Latin America and an "open door" policy elsewhere in the world, ensuring the United States the advantages of imperialism beyond its actual colonies (the Philippines, Puerto Rico, Hawaii). As for Germany and Japan, the drive to catch up with the Atlantic powers by gaining their own colonial empires was a major factor leading to the two world wars. The next great power to industrialize was the Soviet Union. There, it was the internal populations who bore the brunt, in the absence of tropical colonies to exploit. It was all the easier for Western intellectuals to stigmatize Soviet development in that they could compare the situation there with contemporary Britain and France, rather than with their colonies or with the conditions marking their own early industrialization.

When we see that the principal recommendation given by international organisms to Third World countries is to follow the Western example, we can only wonder what on earth they have in mind. Do they want India and Pakistan to solve the Kashmir problem the way France and Germany solved the problem of Alsace-Lorraine? The current development of China, far from being idyllic, is clearly a repetition on a much larger scale of the England of Dickens, with shameless exploitation of workers, child labor, and disruption of the peasantry. The situation is often denounced in the West, but what are they supposed to do? Colonize us?

In the last analysis, the defenders of the dominant discourse on human rights are faced with a dilemma that has no easy solution. On the one hand, they can claim that there is a path to development different from that of the West, one which would respect democracy and human rights. But even leaving aside the problem already mentioned of the exhaustion of resources, which makes it extremely problematic that our lifestyle can be extended to the whole of humanity, it would still be necessary to say a few words to explain just what that path is, and not simply make the assertion.

The other possibility would be to declare that development is of no importance, and all that counts are certain great principles. But the accusation of hypocrisy, which is voiced regularly by Third World leaders, cannot easily be refuted if we are not ready to give up our own standard of living and the political stability that result from centuries of violating those very principles. Now, the least one can say is that giving up their standard of living scarcely seems to be a priority for most of our prominent "human rights defenders."

~

Another Look at Human Rights

To kill 100,000 people because you suspect that the human rights of a few have been denied seems to be a contradiction. Yet the fanaticism of the champions of human rights have led to more people being deprived of their rights, and many of their lives, than the number saved. ...

The people whose hands are soaked in the blood of the innocents, the blood of the Iraqis, the Afghans, the Panamanians, the Nicaraguans, the Chileans, the Ecuadorians; the people who assassinated the presidents of Panama, Chile, Ecuador; the people who ignored international law and mounted military attacks, invading and killing hundreds of Panamanians in order to arrest Noriega and to try him not under Panamanian laws but under their own country's law, have these people a right to question human rights in our country, to make a list and grade the human rights record of the countries of the world yearly, these people with blood-soaked hands?

They have not questioned the blatant abuses of human rights in countries that are friendly to them. In fact, they provide the means for these countries to indulge in human rights abuses.

Israel is provided with weapons, helicopter gunships, bullets coated with depleted uranium, to wage war against people whose only way to retaliate is by committing suicide bombing. ...

But when countries are not friendly with these great powers, their governments claim they have a right to expend money to subvert the government, to support the NGOs to overthrow the government, to ensure only candidates willing to submit to them win. ...

Just as many wrong things are done in the name of Islam and also other religions, worse things are being done in the name of democracy and human rights.

—Former Malaysian prime minister Mohamed Mahathir[23]

∼

I should point out that the critique briefly touched on here goes much more to the heart of the matter than the relatively frequent reproach leveled against the United States for supporting rather systematically dictatorship while claiming to defend democracy. Here it is the *way* we got to the stage where we are now in regard to human rights which ought to be enough to prevent us from giving lessons to the rest of the world.

The Question of Priorities between Types of Rights

In addition to individual and political rights, the 1948 Universal Declaration includes economic and social rights, such as the right to health care, to education, and to social security.[24] Whatever one may think of these rights, they are as much a part of the Declaration and every bit as binding on the signatories as the other rights. Nevertheless, when Jeane Kirkpatrick was Reagan's ambassador to the United Nations, she declared that these rights were "a letter to Santa Claus" without getting much of a rise out of anybody.[25] But how would our press and our intellectuals react if a Third World leader described individual and political rights as a "letter to Santa Claus"?

In the Western mainstream discourse, individual and political rights are considered an absolute priority. The others—economic and social rights—are supposed to follow as countries develop. As we have seen, nothing in the history of the West justifies such an expectation. But this way of setting priorities runs up against other hurdles, which can be illustrated by the example of Cuba.

For some time now, the European left has largely taken up the demand for democratization of Cuba. Let us admit, for the sake of argument, that the Cuban regime is as "totalitarian" as our media claim. Nevertheless, it is perfectly clear that in the rest of Latin America, where the sort of democracy Cuba is exhorted to install already exists, both health care and education are of a notably lower quality and less accessible for the poor majority of the population. If the Cuban public health policy were adopted elsewhere in Latin America, hundreds of thousands of human lives would undoubtedly be saved. It should also be noted that Cuban efforts to provide public health care and education have continued long after the island ceased being "subsidized" by the Soviet Union, and despite being subjected to a severe embargo and countless acts of sabotage caused by the North American superpower, which obviously obliged the Cuban government to allot extra resources to defense, counterespionage, and so on.

This situation confronts the majority of the European left with a serious dilemma. One can always claim that democratization—in the concrete conditions of poor countries under U.S. influence, and given the way the press functions and election campaigns are financed—is not incompatible with access to public health care. But if that is so, why not demand that those politically democratic Latin American countries undertake the necessary reforms to make such access to health care a reality, and why not make this demand with the same fervor with which Cuba is exhorted to become democratic?

~

Elections

It shall be unlawful for a foreign national directly or through any other person to make any contribution of money or other thing of value, or to promise expressly or impliedly to make any such contribution, in connection with an election to any political office or in connection with any primary election,

—United States Code Amended, Article 2, Section 441e (a)

Countries where the United States has intervened to finance particular parties or candidates:[26]

Italy, 1948	Guatemala, 1963	Mongolia, 1996
Philippines, 1950s	Bolivia, 1966	Bosnia, 1998
Lebanon, 1950s	Chile, 1964, 1970	Yugoslavia, 2000
Indonesia, 1955	Italy, 1960–1980s	Nicaragua, 2001
Vietnam, 1955	Portugal, 1974–1975	Bolivia, 2002
British Guyana, 1953–1964	Australia, 1972–1975	Slovakia, 2002
Japan, 1958–1970s	Jamaica, 1976	Georgia, 2003
Nepal, 1959	Panama, 1984, 1989	El Salvador, 2004
Laos, 1960	Nicaragua, 1984, 1990	Afghanistan, 2004
Brazil, 1962	Haiti, 1987–1988	Iraq, 2004
Dominican Republic, 1962	Bulgaria, 1990	Ukraine, 2005
	Russia, 1996	

~

Or else one can admit that the introduction of "real existing" democracy into Cuba would inevitably lead to a capitalist transformation of the economy, complete with IMF requirements, which would end up abolishing free health care for everybody. And thus, a choice must necessarily be made, at least in poor countries, between free health care and a multiparty system. When one observes the evolution of the ex-socialist countries, one can see that the risk is by no means imaginary. But then, in the name of what principle should that choice be made? Are a certain number of political prisoners and a certain degree of censorship and repression worse than thousands of children dying for lack of care? And, perhaps more to the point, should this choice be made by people who for the most part enjoy the benefits of *both* health care *and* democratic freedoms (European intellectuals or the leaders of Reporters Without Borders)? What choice would be made by the two or three billion people living on one or two dollars per day? I don't claim to have a satisfactory answer to these questions, but they are seldom asked, and it is easy to understand why.

It is clear that all the rights included in the 1948 Declaration are desirable. But it is no more legitimate to set aside one part of the Declaration—the part on social and economic rights—than to set aside the other. Moreover, we may think that the existence of political rights leads to social rights. But things are not so simple. Let us just suppose that there exists a planet inhabited by creatures similar to ourselves, but where, following a long historic process in which brute force played a major role, a small number of individuals possess all the wealth, the means of production, and the means of communication. The rest of the population live in abject poverty, without access to education or health care, and work hard to fulfill the desires of those few rich individuals. Free elections are held on that planet, and a few critical but totally marginalized intellectuals are free to express themselves, and yet nothing changes so far as distribution of wealth is concerned. In fact, the small wealthy group, thanks to its control of the media, can repeatedly launch campaigns of intimidation and denigration against all those who would seek to create more equality, and their wealth allows them to buy the politicians and most of the intelligentsia. On that planet, obviously totally different from ours, the part of the Declaration concerning individual and political rights is satisfied. But does that make the situation just or desirable?

It goes without saying that our world is by no means an exact replica of that imaginary planet, despite strong resemblances. Indeed, on our planet one can hope that political rights will eventually make it possible to diminish economic inequalities (as has been accomplished to a certain extent with the development of trade unions and left parties in Europe). But that hope is quite contrary to putting forward political rights to the exclusion of all other considerations.

Before the emergence of the human rights ideology, such remarks were taken for granted by everyone, at least on the left, whatever the tendency, and even by a good part of the right. This is no longer such a sure thing today. Everyone used to agree that survival was the first priority, and that it required a certain social organization, sometimes involving coercion, and that in any case political rights could not really exist unless certain minimal economic conditions were fulfilled. In the words of Berthold Brecht, "First comes eating, then comes morality."[27] Yet even the Stalinist current of the traditional left did not reject individual and political rights on principle as a worthy goal, even though in practice they were postponed indefinitely. The only ideologies that were in real conflict with human rights, even in principle, and not simply as to what needed to be done to achieve them, were certain religious, aristocratic, or communitarian ideologies. The disagreement between Marxism and liberalism, in all their respective forms, had to do with means and priorities, not with desirable goals.

An incident illustrates the radical transformation of the left on the issue of human rights. On a visit to Tunisia, French president Chirac provoked an uproar by declaring that "the very first human rights are to eat, to be cared for, to receive an education and be housed," and in that regard, Tunisia was "way ahead of many other countries," adding that he did not doubt that "the liberal character, respectful of freedoms, was increasingly asserted" in Tunisia. I have no intention of defending that statement in regard to the particular case of Tunisia, but rather point out that the indignant reactions did not clearly distinguish between the particular case and the principle voiced concerning the "first of human rights."[28] Suppose someone says, "Brazil, contrary to Cuba, is a democracy." This sort of statement is not usually considered an apology for the social situation in Brazil and no human rights organization would be shocked or indignant enough to stress that "civil, political, economic, social and cultural rights are indivisible" although, manifestly, economic and social rights are far from being satisfactory in Brazil. But a statement such as that of Chirac's is taken ipso facto as an apology for the political situation in Tunisia and a defense of dictatorship. This difference in reactions reflects the whole difference in the way these two parts of the Declaration are treated. During that visit, even the French Communist Party expressed indignation at Chirac's declaration, although it was merely a very moderate expression of what used to be that party's ideology back in its heyday.[29]

The Question of Relationship of Forces and Our Position in the World

Finally, let us look at the effects of the softest version of the human rights ideology, the one that asks us to write letters or sign petitions in protest against violations of those rights committed in Third World countries. I do not intend here to reject that form of action, which often has positive effects, but simply wish to shed light on certain of its underlying assumptions, which deserve reflection.

Let us consider the following scenario: some citizens of a poor African country undertake to protest en masse against, let us say, human rights violations in China. It is manifestly improbable that such a thing would ever happen and the reason is obvious: the citizens of all such countries know full well that Chinese leaders would pay no attention to such protests, for two reasons—one bad and the other less so. The bad reason is that a poor country obviously has no means of bringing pressure on China. A better reason, that the Chinese could cite, is that the citizens of that African country would do better to solve their own problems before minding other people's business.

It goes without saying that citizens of rich Western countries who protest against such and such a crime committed in some distant country more or less take it for granted that those two objections cannot apply to their initiative. That is partly true, but that is precisely what raises serious problems. First of all, our nations are rich and powerful, both diplomatically and militarily, which is precisely the condition that enables public opinion in these countries to bring pressure. But that means that this public opinion does not essentially exercise its influence directly, for example, by way of contacts with the citizens of the countries concerned by the protests, but indirectly, through the action of governments that are able to take economic sanctions or other harsh measures. And it is this governmental power, which has nothing particularly noble or altruistic about it, which actually lends force to our protests.

Moreover, these protests are not heard mainly in the countries to which they are addressed, China or Iran, for example, but in our own countries and by our own leaders. And if we want to evaluate the probable effect of our actions that is what we must think about first of all. Each protest concerning violations of human rights abroad reinforces, even if unintentionally, the self-satisfaction and good conscience of the West.

As to the second response that the Chinese could make to their imaginary African detractors, "solve your own problems first," almost everyone in our Western countries is convinced that such a response could not be addressed to us. So long as it is limited to the issue of human rights and democracy, that conviction can be defended.[30] But there are still all the problems already mentioned concerning our disproportionate consumption of natural resources, and thus our growing dependence on the very Third World countries whose practices we denounce, not to mention our contribution to global warming. Chinese leaders could very well say that instead of giving them lectures on human rights and democracy, we would do better to start to reform our mode of consumption so as to give the rest of the world a chance to share it, at least in part. And the answer that the defenders of Western interventionism could reasonably give them is far from obvious.

4

Weak and Strong Arguments against War

The anti-apartheid militant Steve Biko used to say that the most powerful weapon in the hands of the oppressor was the mind of the oppressed. One could add that the strength of an ideological system lies in the extent to which its presuppositions are shared by the people who think of themselves as its most radical critics. To allow construction of a more effective opposition to current wars it is necessary to distinguish, among arguments heard against those wars, which ones are solid and which ones are not, and combat the influence of the dominant discourse on the discourse with the opposition. Weak arguments are the those that are based, at least in part, on the suppositions of the dominant discourse.

Weak Arguments

An Italian friend once explained to me that when he was young he thought the revolution could be exported. Today, he no longer thinks so, and by the same token he does not think that democracy can be exported, either. As a result, he is opposed to the war in Iraq. This is a typical example of an extremely widespread line of argument that can be summed up as "it won't work," meaning war won't succeed in installing democracy. It is obviously better to be against the war on those grounds than to be for it, but it's a weak argument on which to base opposition. So let's transpose that argument to other situations: let us imagine, to take an extreme example, that someone said he was against Nazi aggressions because they did not serve to defend Europe from Bolshevism. Or, to take a slightly less extreme case, that someone was against the Soviet invasions of Czechoslovakia in 1968 and of Afghanistan in 1981 because they did not serve to defend socialism. The weakness of the argument appears as soon as it is transposed. It consists in admitting from the outset two things that practically no one concedes in the case of the Nazis or the Soviets: 1) that the reasons proclaimed are the true reasons for going to war; and 2) that the agent who claims to pursue those objectives has the right to do so. And it is precisely this that must be challenged in the case of the United States' wars.

Aside from its morally dubious side, the trouble with the pragmatic argument ("it won't work") is that sometimes it does work, at least in part. In that case, what becomes of the argument against the war? What would there be to say if the Iraqis got discouraged and gave up their resistance, and a stable pro-American government were installed in Baghdad? After all, that is more or less what happened in the case of the Kosovo war: the Albano-Kosovars welcomed NATO as liberators and the Serbs ended up by electing a government that suited their aggressors. To take another example, the U.S. wars of the 1980s in Central America, which cost tens of thousands of lives, did indeed work, in the sense that the populations ended up electing the "right" candidates and that the guerrilla movements were more or less brought to heel.

One can of course reply that the proclaimed objectives are not really achieved: for example, Kosovo is much less multiethnic today than before the war, whereas preserving multiethnicity was supposed to be an objective. But to that, the partisans of intervention will reply that nothing is perfect and it's better to do things halfway than not at all.

Another argument frequently heard, though equally weak, consists in saying that the costs of war (in human life, for example) are too high. But what do you say when high-technology war limits casualties?

Let us consider three examples, two real and one imaginary, which suggest how to answer these questions. First, the Soviet invasion of Czechoslovakia caused very few casualties; second, the annexation of the Sudeten region in that same country by Hitler in 1938 was welcomed by the inhabitants; and finally, let us imagine that the September 11 attacks had taken place in India, whereupon India, a democracy, invaded Afghanistan and Iraq to "liberate" their populations.[1] In the two real cases, the circumstances mentioned certainly did not suffice to justify those aggressions in our eyes, and there is no doubt that, if the imaginary case actually happened, Western opposition to that "liberation" would be overwhelming. One can cite a real example that is comparable: the Vietnamese intervention in Cambodia that overthrew the bloodthirsty regime of Pol Pot and was overwhelmingly condemned by the West. Moreover, a certain number of terrorist attacks have taken place in India, without anyone suggesting that India was thereby authorized to wage an endless war against terrorism in contempt of international law.

These examples indicate that the attitude adopted toward a war or an aggression does not depend solely on the particular situation involved but on more general principles. The first of these principles is international law, such as it exists today, and that can be the basis of strong arguments against recent U.S. wars, none of which was in accordance with international law.[2] Moreover, the law itself is increasingly under attack, among other things precisely because it doesn't provide enough opportunity for unilateral intervention.

Strong Arguments: 1. The Defense of International Law

As is very well explained by the Canadian professor of international law Michael Mandel, contemporary international law has as its aim, to cite the preamble of the United Nations Charter, to "preserve future generations from the scourge of war." And to achieve that, the basic principle is that no country has the right to send its troops into another country without the consent of its government. The Nazis did so repeatedly, and the first crime for which they were condemned at Nuremberg was initiating a war of aggression, which, according to the 1945 Nuremberg Charter, "is the supreme international crime, differing only from other war crimes in that it contains within itself the accumulated evil of the whole."

The "government" whose consent is required does not need to be an "elected government" or one that "respects human rights" but simply has to be whoever "effectively controls the armed forces," because that factor determines whether crossing the border leads to war. It is easy to criticize this basic principle, and the human rights defenders do not fail to do so. For one thing, it is often the case that the borders of states are arbitrary, having resulted from totally undemocratic processes that took place in the distant past, and are considered unsatisfactory by various ethnic minorities. Moreover, nothing ensures that the governments are democratic or even minimally concerned with the welfare of their populations. But international law never claimed to solve all problems. Like practically all law, it seeks simply to be a lesser evil compared to no law at all. And those who criticize international law would do well to explain by which principles they want to have it replaced. Can Iran occupy neighboring Afghanistan? Can Brazil, which is at least as democratic as the United States, invade Iraq in order to install a democracy? Can Congo attack Rwanda in self-defense? Can Bangladesh intervene in the internal affairs of the United States in order to impose a reduction of greenhouse gases so as to "prevent" the devastation with which it is threatened by global warming? If the "preventive" American attack on Iraq was legitimate, why wasn't the Iraqi attack on Iran, or on Kuwait, also legitimate? Worse still, why wasn't the Japanese attack on Pearl Harbor a legitimate preventive attack?[3] When one asks such questions, it quickly becomes clear that the only realistic alternative to the existing law, other than widespread chaos, would be for the most powerful state in the world to intervene wherever it pleases, or else, in some cases, to authorize its allies to do so.

Now, all of liberal thinking since the seventeenth century is based on the idea that there are essentially three forms of life in society:

- the war of all against all
- an absolute sovereign who imposes peace by force
- a legal, democratic order as the lesser evil

Dictatorial regimes, denounced by human rights defenders, have the advantages of the absolute sovereign: ability to preserve order and avoid the war of all against all, which is illustrated today by the situation of so-called failed states. But the drawbacks of such a sovereign are well-known: he acts in accordance with his own interests, his authority is not accepted in the hearts and minds of his subjects, and this provokes an endless cycle of revolts and repression. This observation is the foundation of the argumentation in favor of the third solution.

All that is considered banal when it is a matter of the internal order of democratic states. But now let us turn to the international order. The sovereign, should we abandon the existing principles of international law, would inevitably be the United States. The United States is a great power that obviously pursues its own interests. Let us note that the advocates of humanitarian intervention do not always deny that fact, but then they argue, by recourse to a selective reading of history, that the rest of humanity gains more benefits than harm from that pursuit. I have already tried to explain why I do not share that conclusion, but however that may be, the backlash linked to the exercise of that absolute power is exactly what classic liberalism predicted.[4]

Examples are easy to find. Osama bin Laden is a product of the support provided to the mujahiddin in Afghanistan during the Soviet period. By selling weapons to Iraq, the West inadvertently provided a precious aid to the present Iraqi resistance.

In 1954, the United States overthrew Arbenz in Guatemala. For Washington, it took little effort and, apparently, involved little risk. However, the United States thereby also contributed to the political education of a young Argentine doctor who happened to be there and whose portrait today adorns millions of T-shirts throughout the world: Che Guevara.

After the First World War, a young Vietnamese came to the Versailles Conference to plead the cause of self-determination for his people to Robert Lansing, secretary of state of the president who presented himself as the champion of self-determination, Woodrow Wilson. He was shown the door; after all, he was harmless.[5] He then left France for Moscow to complete his political education and became famous. His name was Ho Chi Minh.

Who knows what the hatred being produced today by the policies of the United States and Israel will give birth to tomorrow?

In the international order, the third solution, the liberal solution, would mean more democracy at the world level, through the United Nations. Bertrand Russell compared discussing who was responsible for the First World War to discussing who was responsible for a car accident in a country without traffic regulations. The mere awareness of the idea that international law should be respected and that it should be possible to control conflicts between states through an international entity is in itself a major step in human history, comparable to the abolition of the power of the monarchy and the aristocracy, the abolition of slavery, the development of freedom of expression, recognition of trade union and women's rights, or the concept of social security. At present, it is obviously the United States, as well as those who support their actions in the name of human rights, who are opposed to strengthening that international order. And there is every reason to fear that the reforms of the United Nations that are currently under consideration will lead to a greater legitimization of unilateral actions. The problem with the idea of using human rights to undermine the international order is that, at every meeting of the nonaligned countries, and at every summit of Southern Hemisphere countries, which represent 70 percent of humanity, all forms of unilateral intervention, whether embargos, sanctions or wars, are condemned, and not only by "dictatorships." The same thing occurs during votes in the U.N. General Assembly, concerning the U.S. embargo against Cuba, for example. The democracy argument, if what is meant by that is to take into account world public opinion, weighs massively against the right of unilateral intervention. In the last analysis, the liberal imperialists, that is, most of the U.S. Democrats and a large part of European social democrats and greens—who defend democracy on the domestic level but call for intervention, that is, the dictatorship of a sole country or small group of countries, on the international level—are perfectly incoherent.

The most frequently heard argument is that it is scandalous for the United Nations, and particularly its Human Rights Commission, to treat democratic and undemocratic countries as equals. But in democracy there is no morality test for voting, and citizens' rights do not depend on the quality of their family life. Nations, like individuals, can change and improve their behavior, and need a certain amount of time and space to do so without violent intrusions. Besides, nothing proves that the most powerful state is best able to judge the internal virtues and vices of others, as it presumes to do—always giving the highest marks to itself. The fact that the United States can present itself as the universal arbiter of respect for human rights, at the same time it holds prisoners for years in Guantánamo without trial or even formal charges, shows that a government's attitude toward human rights in the context of the Human Rights Commission may be disconnected from its own practice.

~

The Movement of Non-Aligned Countries and the United Nations

The Heads of State or Government reaffirmed the Movement's commitment to enhance international co-operation to resolve international problems of a humanitarian character in full compliance with the Charter of the

United Nations, and, in this regard, they reiterated the rejection by the
Non-Aligned Movement of the so-called "right" of humanitarian intervention, which has no basis either in the Charter of the United Nations or in
international law.[6]

~

Finally, when, as often happens, people complain of the United Nations'
lack of effectiveness, it is necessary to recall all the treaties and all the agreements on disarmament or on prohibition of weapons of mass destruction
opposed primarily by the United States. It is the great powers who are most
hostile to the idea that their trump card, recourse to force, might encounter
legal opposition. But just as on the domestic level nobody suggests that
gangsters' hostility to the law is a good argument for abolishing it, the sabotage of the United Nations by the United States is not a valid argument for
discrediting the world organization.

~

The United States and Weapons Proliferation

The Bush administration has withdrawn from the Kyoto Protocol , opposed
the International Plan for Cleaner Energy, withdrawn from the International
Conference on Racism, refused to join 123 nations pledged to ban the use
and production of anti-personnel bombs and mines, opposed the UN
Agreement to Curb the International Flow of Illicit Small Arms, refused to
accept the 1972 Biological and Toxin Weapons Convention, refused to join
the International Court of Justice, withdrawn from the 1972 Anti-Ballistic
Missiles Treaty, rejected the Comprehensive [Nuclear] Test Ban Treaty,
among other matters. It is developing more refined nuclear weapons for
more practical use, is pursuing space-based weapons stations, and has
announced a right to engage in preventive war at its own discretion.

—Edward S. Herman[7]

~

But there is one more argument in favor of international law, perhaps even more important than the others: it is the paper shield that the Third World believed could protect it from the West at the time of decolonization. People who use human rights to undermine international law in the name of the "right to intervene" forget that, all through the colonial period, no border and no dictator was there to prevent the West from making human rights prevail in the countries it had subjected. If that was the intention, the least one can say is that the colonialized peoples failed to notice. And this is probably one of the main reasons why the right to intervene is so strongly condemned by the countries of the South.

~

East Timor and the United Nations

When, in December 1975, Indonesia invaded the former Portuguese colony of East Timor, which had just gained its independence, the United Nations remained powerless, something for which it is bitterly reproached in other cases, for instance Bosnia. But why was it ineffective? The U.S. ambassador to the United Nations at the time, Daniel Patrick Moynihan, explained in his memoirs: "The Department of State desired that the United Nations prove utterly ineffective in whatever measures it undertook. This task was given to me, and I carried it forward with no inconsiderable success." A little further on, he explained that the invasion was responsible for the death of "10 percent of the population, almost the proportion of casualties experienced by the Soviet Union during the Second World War."[8] That same year Moynihan, who boasts of having collaborated with a massacre that he himself compares to those caused by Hitler's aggression, was awarded the highest distinction of the International League of Human Rights. More recently, in 2002, he was one of the sixty signatories of a "Letter from America: The Reasons for a Combat" which argued in favor of the invasion of Afghanistan as a just war.[9]

The United States and the United Nations

On the occasion of the United Nations condemnation of the U.S. invasion of the small Caribbean island of Grenada in 1983, President Reagan declared:"One hundred nations in the U.N. have not agreed with us on just about everything that's come before them where we're involved, and it didn't upset my breakfast at all."

Here is a small sampling of U.N. General Assembly resolutions; the figures indicate the number of states having voted in favor and those voting against, identified in parentheses:

• December 11, 1980: Israeli human rights practices in occupied territories: 118–2 (United States, Israel).

• December 12, 1980: Declaration of non-use of nuclear weapons against non-nuclear states: 110–2 (United States, Albania).

• October 28, 1981: Antiracism; condemns apartheid in South Africa and Namibia: 145–1 (United States).

• December 9, 1981: Establishment of a nuclear-weapon-free zone in the Middle East: 107–2 (United States, Israel).

• December 14, 1981: Declares that education, work, health care, proper nourishment, national development, etc., are human rights: 135–1 (United States).

• December 9, 1982: Promoting international mobilization against apartheid: 141–1 (United States).

• December 13, 1982: Necessity of a convention on the prohibition of chemical and bacteriological weapons: 95–1 (United States).

• November 22, 1983: The right of every state to choose its economic and social system in accord with the will of its people, without outside interference in whatever form it takes: 131–1 (United States).

In addition, year after year, resolutions adopted calling for an end to the U.S. embargo against Cuba have been adopted by huge majorities, with only the United States and Israel voting against, on a few occasions joined by Albania, Paraguay, or Uzbekistan.[10]

~

2. An Anti-imperialist Perspective

An Argentinian friend said to me one day that without its foreign debt, his country would be "a paradise." He may have been exaggerating, but I immediately asked him, "Why then do you continue to pay it?" Everyone in Argentina knows that the debt is largely illegitimate, at least the part inherited from the time of the dictators. He replied, "But they would laugh at us if we did not." By "they" he obviously meant the United States and the U.S.-supported financial institutions. But what could those institutions do about it?

More generally, what would happen if a country put into practice the ideas of various anti-globalization or "global justice" movements? Not only measures such as the "Tobin tax" which, depending on how it was defined, might possibly be integrated into the system without too much trouble, but more radical measures such as widespread debt repudiation, reappropriation of natural resources, (re)construction of strong public services, significant taxation of profits, etc. I see no reason to believe that the reaction would be very different from what it was with Allende, Castro, Mossadegh, Lumumba, Arbenz, Goulart, and many others. The reaction would occur in stages: first of all, more or less spontaneous economic sabotage, in the form of capital flight, a stop to investments, credit, and "aid," etc. Should that not suffice, there would be encouragement of internal subversion, provoked by social, ethnic, or religious groups with specific demands difficult to satisfy. Any repression of those groups, even if their activities were illegal and would be equally repressed anywhere else, would be condemned in the name of human rights. The economic or political complexity of the situation would be forgotten. All this would take place under constant threat of a military coup d'état, which could be welcomed by a part of the population tired of "chaos." And, if all that should fail to do the trick, the United States or its allies would resort to direct military intervention. The point is that even if the last measure is not taken the moment each new crisis arises, it nevertheless looms in the background of all the others. If economic sanctions or internal destabilization measures don't work, one can expect a new Bay of Pigs, a new Vietnam, or new Contras.

~

The Contras and Human Rights Defenders

After the victory of the Sandinistas in Nicaragua in 1979, which overthrew the U.S.-supported dictatorship of Somoza, the United States decreed an embargo against Nicaragua and organized guerrilla bands called Contras. They had no chance of winning a military victory, but they could weaken the new government, especially by disrupting the economy. In 1990, the Sandinistas lost the elections, whereupon the United States lifted their embargo. The United States was condemned for its sabotage actions by the International Court of Justice in 1986. Despite a demand by the U.N. General Assembly for immediate payment of reparations, the United States refused to comply.

The United States can, however, count on its own lobby of European intellectuals. On March 21, 1985, the leading French newspaper, Le Monde, published a paid advertisement on page 6 calling on the U.S. Congress to aid "all sectors of the opposition" in Nicaragua, that is, the Contras in particular, against "a totalitarian party"—the Sandinistas.

This aid, according to the text, was necessary for "strategic" reasons; "the Sandinista junta has never hidden its aim to integrate all of Central America into a single Marxist-Leninist entity."[11] If this should happen, the United States "would be obliged to disengage from one of their principal overseas treaties, and that is precisely the objective sought by Soviet strategy: to force the United States to withdraw from regions of vital importance to both the USSR and the Free World."

The alarmed signatories included some big names in French intellectual circles, among them Fernando Arrabal, playwright; Eugene Ionesco, playwright; Bernard-Henri Lévy, philosopher; Jean-François Revel, writer; Olivier Todd, journalist, writer; Emmanuel Le Roy-Ladurie, historian; Vladimir Bukovsky; Simon Wiesenthal.

Aside from their strategic acumen, these thinkers had a moral argument: "The West must be consistent in its support to those who fight to benefit from the rights that your own Declaration of Independence proclaimed inalienable, and which therefore should belong to all."

It may be noted that the Sandinistas overthrew a dictatorship, organized and won the first democratic elections in their country, lost the second elections, and left office. Hardly a model "totalitarian party."

On the other hand, a 1984 CIA "Psychological Operations" manual destined for "freedom fighters," as Reagan called the Contras, included the following recommendations:

> Kidnap all officials or agents of the Sandinista government. ...
>
> It is possible to neutralize carefully selected and planned targets, such as court judges, mesta judges [justices of the peace], police and State Security officials, Sandinista Defense Committee chiefs, etc. ...
>
> The notification of the police denouncing a target who does not want to join the guerrillas, can be carried out easily ... through a letter with false statements of citizens who are not implicated in the movement. ...
>
> If possible; professional criminals will be hired to carry out specific selected "jobs."

A shorter manual in comic book form recommended "a series of useful sabotage techniques" to hasten "liberation":

Stop up toilets with sponges ... pull down power cables ... put dirt into gas tanks ... put nails on roads and highways ... telephone to make false hotel reservations and false alarms of fires and crimes ... hoard and steal food from the government ... leave lights and water taps on ... steal mail from mailboxes ... rip up books ... spread rumors.[12]

Thus was brought to an end an original and democratic attempt at social transformation, and to what Oxfam called "the threat of the good example."

~

As a matter of fact, the electorate, especially the poor, understand these things quite well. That is why they are often more easily won over by "providential" leaders than by the political left. A populist demagogue may be able to bring about temporary improvements within the system without provoking the anger of those who hold real power on the world scale. In Third World countries, fundamental changes would be in the interest of a large majority of the population. But so long as the left fails to offer a credible explanation of how it would overcome the obstacles it would have to confront if it came to power by democratic means, it will have a lot of trouble getting there. To put it another way, all elections are distorted by a permanent and implicit blackmail: if you vote for an authentic left, you will have to take the consequences.

The key to the whole system, that which ensures the effectiveness of indirect interventions, or what can be called low-intensity interventions, is the immense military power of the United States and its allies. Moreover, they are the ones who arm and train numerous Third World armies, which often hang as a sword of Damocles over any attempt at social transformation. That is why the social justice movement in its opposition to neoliberal globalization cannot reasonably fail to adopt an anti-interventionist and anti-imperialist attitude. The process under way in Venezuela has already had to withstand economic sabotage and electoral destabilization in an attempted coup d'état. It has survived up to now, but who knows for how long. In any case, Hugo Chávez certainly understands the connection between social reforms and opposition to imperialism, since he organized an anti-imperialist tribunal during the world festival of youth and students in Caracas, in August 2005.

~

Racism and Pseudo-scientific Jargon

The inventors of chaos theory were poets, precisely because they were great mathematicians. Thus we owe to them the metaphor, which has become famous, according to which the fluttering of a butterfly's wings in one part of the world can provoke a hurricane at the other end of the earth. Behind that admirable comparison, the point is that complex causalities are at work in nature, in which apparently insignificant objects can, by their own force, if inserted in a devastating mechanism, have effects completely out of proportion to their initial importance. . . .

In Latin America, we are currently on the eve of such a situation, but less poetic and more brutal metaphors come to mind to express the same catastrophe theory, for instance that the brusque crack of a primate's jaw can provoke a volcanic eruption. The primate or gorilla, you'll have recognized, is the apprentice dictator of Venezuela, Chávez; and the volcanic eruption is obviously a general confrontation embracing the whole continent, for the first time in its history, of which one possible consequence will be fresh tension on oil and commodity markets, and another, the most thorough preparation of an unprecedented geopolitical tension between China and the United States.[13]

~

In the last analysis, opposition to recent wars can be based not only on the idea that international law is the sole means of avoiding a state of war of all against all or the dictatorship of a single country, but also because the

United States is systematically hostile to all serious social progress in the Third World and that, as a result, any such progress presupposes a weakening of U.S. power.

5

Illusions and Mystifications

Unfortunately, the intrinsic problem is not only a matter of good and bad arguments but of non-arguments, that is, of frequently repeated ideas whose consequences are rarely made explicit but nevertheless produce a demobilizing effect within antiwar movements. First, there are a certain number of illusions current in progressive movements; then, there are various devices to give "pacifists" a bad conscience, unfortunately often internalized.

Anti-fascist Fantasies

When Lebanon was invaded in 1982, an Israeli opposed to that war, Uri Avnery, wrote an open letter to Menahem Begin titled: "Mr. Prime Minister, Hitler Is dead."[1] This was because Begin claimed to be attacking the "new Hitler," meaning Arafat, entrenched in Beirut. Ever since the Suez Canal crisis, when Nasser was "Hitler on the Nile," every adversary of the West—Saddam, Milosevic, the Islamists—is a "new Hitler," "green fascist," etc. One can observe that whenever the comparison is reversed, clumsily in my opinion (Bush or Sharon equals Hitler), it is met with accusations of trivializing Nazism. Of course, before there was Hitler, each new enemy—the

Germans during the First World War, for example—were the new Huns, led by a new Attila, and this type of rhetoric can simply be dismissed as low-level war propaganda.

Nevertheless, beyond this rhetoric there is a vision of the Second World War that plays a major role in legitimizing war. The general idea is that the West, by cowardice or indifference, waited too long to launch a preventive war against Hitler that would have saved the Jews. This argument is psychologically particularly effective, and particularly vicious, when it is used against people of the generation that grew up in the 1960s and felt that the crimes committed against the Jews had not been sufficiently recognized immediately after 1945.

~

The New Anti-Semitism

America's antiwar movement, still puny and struggling, is showing signs of being hijacked by one of the oldest and darkest prejudices there is. Perhaps it was inevitable. The conflict against Islamo-fascism obviously circles back to the question of Israel. Fanatical anti-Semitism, as bad or even worse than Hitler's, is now a cultural norm across the Middle East. It's the acrid glue that unites Saddam, Arafat, Al-Qaeda, Hezbollah, Iran, and the Saudis.

—Andrew Sullivan[2]

~

New wars are repeatedly justified by analogy with that situation: we must save the Albano-Kosovars, the Kurds (in Iraq, but not in Turkey), Afghan women, etc. During the Kosovo war, I constantly ran up against that argument—but shouldn't we have declared war on Hitler in 1936?— even from political militants whose supposedly "Marxist" background should have led to more lucidity. The Kosovo example is an illustration of how the use of analogy often enables people to dispense with informing themselves seriously about the realities of a given situation.

We may observe in passing that in the view of classic political liberalism, war strengthens the powers of the state and should be avoided except in cases of extreme necessity. Trade negotiations and cultural exchanges are far preferable to war or to embargoes. The whole ideology of the "new Hitlers" goes against these liberal ideas, and thus is more often adopted by ex-revolutionaries who have renounced their past, retaining only a certain anti-liberal sympathy for violent change. This ideology gives intellectuals a role to play, mobilizing public opinion "before it's too late."

There are two answers to this argument, one conceptual, the other historic. The conceptual aspect, that is, the defense of international law in the face of legitimization of preventive war, which constitutes the principal aspect of the response, has already been mentioned. The historic aspect has to do with what really happened before and during the Second World War. It deserves to be recalled, inasmuch as the reference to those events to justify military intervention is symptomatic of a widespread ignorance, or a radical revision, of history. Here we shall be brief, since a treatise on history is beyond the scope of this book.

"Better Hitler than the Popular Front" was a slogan that expressed the attitude not only of the defeatist segment of the French bourgeoisie, frightened by the success of the left in the mid-1930s, but also, each in its own way, of a good part of the British aristocracy, of the American capitalist class and of the dominant social classes throughout Europe. If there was no war against Hitler, it was, among other things, because the "social achievements" of fascism—eliminating left-wing parties and disciplining the workers thanks to corporatism and nationalism—won the admiration of the dominant social classes everywhere, the very counterparts of those who today call for preventive wars against new Hitlers. This being the case, a defensive alliance against Hitler—such as the one that fought in 1914–18, but with the Soviet Union replacing tsarist Russia—capable of preventing World War II altogether by dissuading aggression, was out of the question precisely because of the anticommunism of the ruling circles in the West. Moreover, avoiding war is what would have made it possible to save most of the Jews, since it was only after the war was well under way that they were massively killed. Western government aid to the Spanish Republic, whose victory, had it taken place, might well have served to dampen the ambitions of fascism, was impossible for the same reasons. It should be emphasized that neither a defensive alliance nor aid to a legal government violates international law, in contrast to a preventive attack. Moreover, the Munich Agreement that allowed Hitler to seize the Sudetenland was not merely a matter of cowardice, but was also due to hostility toward Czechoslovakia, the European country most favorable to an alliance with the Soviet Union.

The discourse on the "new Hitlers" is inevitably accompanied by the more or less explicit identification of today's pacifists with Daladier and Chamberlain. But apart from misrepresentation of the motivations of the "appeasers," the logical lesson from Munich is not that we should plunge madly into war on all sides to defend minorities, which was precisely what Hitler claimed he was doing. Hitler legitimized his wars as the necessary way to protect minorities, first the Sudeten Germans in Czechoslovakia and then the Germans in Danzig. Note also that at the end of the Second World War, the United Nations was set up precisely to ban "preventive war," a notion that Eisenhower, for example, viewed as essentially Nazi.

The logical lesson of Munich is that the great power gambit of using the discontents of minorities to destabilize weaker countries is extremely dangerous, at least for world peace, even when the minorities in question welcome such great power intervention, as the Sudeten Germans welcomed Nazi Germany in 1938 and the Kosovo Albanians welcomed NATO in 1999. The fact is that "liberating" the Sudeten Germans encouraged Hitler just as "saving" Kosovo gave American imperialism a huge bonus in legitimacy.

The catastrophe of Hitler's victory over France in 1940 finally led part of Europe's ruling circles to fall back on an alliance with the Soviet Union, though too late to avoid the war, too late to avoid the suffering it inflicted on the victims of aggression, and too late to avoid paying the political price that inevitably resulted from the victory over fascism that was primarily due to the Red Army and the sacrifices of the Soviet people. The visionaries who attack "pacifists" by harping on the 1930s would do well to study those years a bit more thoroughly.

Defenders of humanitarian war in Iraq stress the inconsistency of those who oppose such a war in Iraq when they agreed to it in Yugoslavia.[3] They are obviously right on this point, and therefore one of the main reasons to oppose the 1999 war was precisely that, by agreeing to it, we were de facto legitimizing an indefinite number of other wars. The endless war in which we are involved today is in part the consequence of the euphoria brought about by the easy victory over Yugoslavia in 1999.

Finally, if playing the little game that consists in saying, once it is known how history turned out, "Ah, if only at such and such a time one had done this or that" (for instance, launch a war against Hitler in 1936), one might as well ask whether it wouldn't have been a good idea to avoid the First World War. In those days, there was neither Hitler, nor Stalin, nor Milosevic, nor Saddam Hussein. The world was dominated, as it still is today, by governments that are imperialist in their foreign policy but relatively liberal in domestic policy. Nevertheless, this liberalism in no way prevented an accumulation of weaponry on all sides, secret treaties, colonial wars. A spark in Sarajevo and Europe was plunged into a war that dragged the world after it, and whose unexpected results included the emergence of both Bolshevism and fascism. Those who ceaselessly decry the "tragedies of the twentieth century" would do well to reflect on their origins and on the similarity between the interventionist policies and the search for hegemony that they advocate today and the policies that led to the catastrophe of the summer of 1914.

It can be suggested that if World War I is largely forgotten, this is not only because it took place further back in time than World War II. Indeed, the more time passes, the more the Second World War seems to gain importance—in any case, as presented through the dominant interpretation discussed above (sixty years after the end of the First World War, we were in 1978. Who in 1978 was still thinking about the First World War?). The fundamental reason is no doubt that the First World War was the epitome of a totally absurd war. There was no valid reason to wage it in the first place, and the "victory" only gave birth to new problems. The Versailles Treaty, mainly sought by French leaders to protect France by crushing Germany once and for all, is a perfect example of human passions producing the opposite result of the one intended: Germany relentlessly took its revenge, which led to France's defeat in 1940 and the beginning of the end of its role as a great power. In contrast, thanks to Hitler's unilateral aggression, the Second World War remains the most justifiable of all wars, at least for the countries he attacked. As a result, constant reference to the Second World War is used to strengthen the case for war, whereas lucid reflection on the First World War would rather be an incitement to pacifism. This partly explains the difference between the way the two are treated.

More generally, there is a pernicious tendency in human psychology to want to "solve" the problems of the past. Sixty years after the fall of Hitler, the "struggle against fascism" and the demand for "vigilance" lest it reassert itself often illustrate this tendency. The deplorable result of this attitude is that horrific atrocities committed by the Americans in Iraq, for example, the destruction of the city of Fallujah, arouse much less attention and protest in France than, for instance, some provocative but inconsequential remark by Jean-Marie Le Pen.

The European Illusion

One of the most dangerous illusions afflicting European progressive, ecological, and peace movements is the belief that if only Europe could strengthen its defense and unify, it could serve as a counterweight to the

United States. To start with, it is high time to stop using euphemisms such as "defense." A recent recruitment poster for the Belgian army explained better than any number of speeches what that word means today: it showed soldiers inspecting documents of Afghan civilians. "Territorial defense" is carried out today thousands of miles away from our own territory. If we really want to speak of defense, and not of humanitarian intervention, we need to know against whom we are defending ourselves and what attack scenario is conceivable.

The other problem is that Europe is playing more or less the same role vis-à-vis the Third World that the United States played just after the Second World War. After 1945, the Americans favored the transition from colonialism to neocolonialism, which allowed them to appear as the "good guys" in contrast to the wicked European colonialists, as during the Suez Crisis in 1956. The "anti-American" faction in European ruling circles would no doubt like to regain lost influence by turning the tables again. This naturally leads them to remind everybody that we Europeans, contrary to the Americans, are really civilized and really respect human rights. A good part of the agitation for worldwide abolition of the death penalty (enacted fairly recently in European countries but quickly adopted as a sort of symbol of Europe's superior moral identity) carries exactly this message. However, the structure of our European societies is too similar to that of the United States and our dependence on the Third World is evolving in ways too similar to theirs for this type of consideration to be anything other than a new "improved" version of "human rights" designed to justify hegemony. Of course, an analogous discourse in the United States serves to assert moral superiority by harping on Germany's Nazi past and identifying France with the Vichy regime.

Europe faces a dilemma. Either it unifies its foreign policy, achieving what was to a great extent the original project of its founders: to avoid self-destructive internal wars and recover its role of imperial power, and leaving leadership in international and military affairs to the United States. This was roughly the attitude of British ruling circles after the loss of their empire, and of German ruling circles after their defeat. Or else Europe really becomes a superpower, and then it would inevitably come into conflict with the United States. This is doubtless the dream of a faction of European elites, fed up with American arrogance, but is extremely difficult to achieve because of the strong political and media influence of the United States in most European countries, not to mention their interlocking military forces and industries. But suppose this dream came true? What would be the benefits? A new arms race, risks of armed conflict, a new Cold War? What was said earlier about the nature of armies, and the impossibility of using them for humanitarian purposes, applies to all armies, including even a future European army.

On the other hand, France's opposition to the invasion of Iraq in 2003 demonstrated that a European country, acting independently of European Union political structures, could perfectly well, if it had the courage, contribute a symbolic support to all those opposed to American hegemony, and without firing a single shot.

~

Europe and the Failed Putsch against Chávez

From April 11 to 14, 2002, Venezuela was the scene of one of the most ephemeral coups d'état in history, rapidly brought to an end by a wave of popular support that threw out the putschists and brought Hugo Chávez back to power. During that short-lived coup d'état, the Spanish presidency of the European Union rushed to issue a statement of which the conclusion says a lot about the democratic sensibilities of certain Europeans: "Finally, the European Union manifests its confidence in the transition government [meaning the putschists] concerning respect for democratic values and institutions, so that the current crisis may be overcome in the framework of a national concertation and with full respect for fundamental rights and freedoms."

A few days later, after the putsch collapsed, the European Union adopted a text that welcomed "the restoration of democratic institutions" while
expressing its "preoccupation in the face of actions undertaken [by the
Chávez government] against national and foreign economic interests."[4]

〜

The Question of Internationalism

The partisans of intervention sometimes portray themselves as carrying on
the noble tradition of left internationalism, but cured of the blindness of
Western communists regarding the USSR, China, Cuba, etc. There is nevertheless a vast difference between that traditional internationalism and the
current ideology. In the original labor, socialist, communist, or Third World
movements, internationalism and solidarity were forms of enlightened self-
interest, the idea being that a community of workers or colonized peoples
had interests in common and they should unite to defend them. There, at
least, the problem of hypocrisy did not arise. Besides, political objectives
unified those movements, such as socialism or decolonization. But what, in
terms of political objectives, does the left today have in common with the
Dalai Lama, the Kosovo Liberation Army, Chechen separatists, Natan
Sharansky, and Vaclav Havel? The left cannot have much in common with
extreme nationalists, mystics, or staunch supporters of the United States or
Israeli colonization. Nevertheless, at one point or another, those individuals
and movements have enjoyed strong support from the Western left.

〜

Vaclav Havel

Vaclav Havel, for example, has no problem when it comes to ignoring victims so long as his political friends are responsible for their fate. Shortly after
six intellectuals engaged in a nonviolent struggle in El Salvador (as he had
done in Czechoslovakia) were assassinated by an army totally dependent

on the United States, he declared in an address to the U.S. Congress that the U.S. superpower was the great "defender of freedom," which predictably won him warm applause.

Our "Dissidents" and Theirs

If Lech Walesa had been doing his organizing work in El Salvador, he would already have entered into the ranks of the disappeared—at the hands of "heavily armed men dressed in civilian clothes"; or have been blown to pieces in a dynamite attack on his union headquarters. If Alexander Dubcek were a politician in our country, he would have been assassinated like Hector Oquelí [the social democratic leader assassinated in Guatemala by Salvadoran death squads according to the Guatemalan government]. If Andrei Sakharov had worked here in favor of human rights, he would have met the same fate as Herbert Anaya [one of the many murdered leaders of the independent Salvadoran Human Rights Commission, CDHES]. If Ota-Sik or Vaclav Havel had been carrying out their intellectual work in El Salvador, they would have [been found] one sinister morning, lying on the patio of a university campus with their heads destroyed by the bullets of an elite army battalion.[5]

∼

Obviously, one can defend the basic rights, such as equality before the law, of political adversaries as well as of friends, but that is no reason to forget the distinction between the two. Besides, one should realize that movements that complain of being persecuted, for example by governments emerging from decolonization, are not always seeking equal rights but sometimes the restoration of former inequalities (a typical example of this phenomenon was the Katangan secession following the independence of the Belgian Congo in 1960). This is the type of distinction that was fundamental for left internationalism, and the disappearance of that distinction is the sign of a grave depoliticization in which good feelings can overrule enlightened self-interest, not out of altruism but simply from lack of lucidity.

The other problem raised by assimilating the present situation to past internationalism is that, for the European left, all references to the interests of the nation have become practically synonymous with fascism. Oddly enough, only minorities have the right to display nationalist sentiments. Stigmatization of "nationalism" is used constantly to condemn any serious criticism of the political direction taken by the European Union; for example, during the 2005 referendum in France on the EU Treaty in which the voters—notably on the left—defied their political leaders and the media to reject a text they judged harmful to their interests. The voters' reluctance to sacrifice hard-won social and economic rights was condemned as nationalism. But the "nationalism" of a people that wants to protect advantages gained in decades of struggle for progress is not comparable to the nationalism of a great power that takes the form of military intervention at the other end of the earth. Moreover, if it is true that national sovereignty does not necessarily bring democracy, there can be no democracy without it.

Finally, certain radical forms of contemporary internationalism illustrate the dangers posed by misuse of Utopianism. Obviously, a world without borders is desirable, but everyone must know that it will not be achieved in the foreseeable future. And least of all in a world at war. Now, insofar as the present "internationalist" ideology tends to scorn the principle of national sovereignty, it tends to encourage interventions in all directions and underestimates the negative effects that intervention can provoke.

To Sign or Not to Sign Petitions

In 2004, two international political petitions were circulated in progressive circles in Europe. One of them exhorted Americans to vote for Kerry against Bush, and the other called on Venezuelans to support Chávez in the referendum on his recall. In both cases, I refused to sign, because both cases illustrated a tendency to assume that national sovereignty has already been more or less abolished, well before such a thing has happened, and before the progressives who make the assumption have really thought it through.

Concerning the petition for Kerry, there were several reasons not to sign it. To start with, in terms of foreign policy, it was by no means so obvious that Kerry was preferable to Bush. His program was at least as militarist as that of Bush, and he had the drawback of being a much more clever speaker. Next, assuming it would be read in the United States, that petition could only be counterproductive. No nation in the world today is more attached to its own sovereignty than the United States, and any attempt to influence its voters is seen as intolerable interference. Moreover, one of the themes of Republican propaganda against Kerry was that he was too "French." It's hard to see how reinforcing that notion would do him any good. This example should indicate to those who consider national sovereignty a thing of the past just how much it has not vanished from today's world but has simply become the privilege of rich countries.

However, the main reason not to sign was that the very attitude of pinning the hopes of the world on Kerry being elected was mistaken. The United States is a sovereign nation and if its voters want to adopt an economic policy leading to their own impoverishment, they have every right to do so. The problem for the rest of the world stems from the United States' perpetual interference in the domestic affairs of other states. What should be done is to build, through appropriate alliances, a system of international relations that limits that interference, and not pray for the Americans to finally elect a benevolent prince. Many Europeans regret that the rest of the world can't take part in American elections; but the unworkable nature of that wish illustrates perfectly the error of those who dismiss national sovereignty, as well as the fact that democracy, which they regard with such reverence, presupposes sovereignty as a necessary condition. It is not up to us to vote in the United States, but it is not up to them to decide how the rest of the world should live. To go a bit further, one can suggest that the hoopla in favor of Kerry was essentially for domestic consumption: to rally European partisans of a "moderate" American imperialism and spread the idea that there exists a "good America," incarnated by the Democrats, who will eventually come back to power one fine day.

The Chávez case was quite different: not voting for him would have been a form of capitulation by the poor majority in Venezuela in the face of internal and external pressures, a bit like what happened in the elections in which the Sandinistas lost power in Nicaragua. My refusal to sign was because I asked myself the following question: Who am I to tell the Venezuelans not to capitulate? Just imagine, as is always possible (think of Chile), that the Americans finally succeed in defeating Chávez by provoking a coup d'état, a civil war, or a conflict with Colombia. It will be the Venezuelans and not I who will have to bear the consequences. What gives me the right to advise them to take such a risk? On the other hand, if they should capitulate in elections, like the Nicaraguans, or through "peace accords," like the Palestinians at Oslo, one can be sure that the majority of the established Western left will celebrate a new "victory of democracy." But count me out: real democracy presupposes a lot of things, including genuine sovereignty, which is incompatible with the multiple forms of blackmail exercised on the voters (from Nicaragua to Ukraine), principally by the United States and by international financial bodies.

~

American Liberals as Bush's "Useful Idiots"

For what distinguishes the worldview of Bush's liberal supporters from that of his neoconservative allies is that they don't look on the "War on Terror," or the war in Iraq, or the war in Lebanon and eventually Iran, as mere serial exercises in the reestablishment of American martial dominance. They see them as skirmishes in a new global confrontation: a Good Fight, reassuringly comparable to their grandparents' war against Fascism and their Cold War liberal parents' stance against international Communism. Once again, they assert, things are clear. The world is ideologically divided; and—as before— we must take our stand on the issue of the age. Long nostalgic for the comforting verities of a simpler time, today's liberal intellectuals have at last discovered a sense of purpose: they are at war with "Islamo-fascism."

Thus Paul Berman, a frequent contributor to *Dissent, The New Yorker,* and other liberal journals, and until now better known as a commentator on American cultural affairs, recycled himself as an expert on Islamic fascism (itself a new term of art), publishing *Terror and Liberalism* just in time for the Iraq war. Peter Beinart, a former editor of *The New Republic,* followed in his wake this year with *The Good Fight: Why Liberals—and Only Liberals—Can Win the War on Terror and Make America Great Again,* where he sketches at some length the resemblance between the War on Terror and the early Cold War. Neither author had previously shown any familiarity with the Middle East, much less with the Wahhabi and Sufi traditions on which they pronounce with such confidence.

But like Christopher Hitchens and other former left-liberal pundits now expert in "Islamo-fascism," Beinart and Berman and their kind really are conversant—and comfortable—with a binary division of the world along ideological lines. In some cases they can even look back to their own youthful Trotskyism when seeking a template and thesaurus for world-historical antagonisms. In order for today's "fight" (note the recycled Leninist lexicon of conflicts, clashes, struggles, and wars) to make political sense, it too must have a single universal enemy whose ideas we can study, theorize, and combat; and the new confrontation must be reducible, like its 20th-century predecessor, to a familiar juxtaposition that eliminates exotic complexity and confusion: Democracy v. Totalitarianism, Freedom v. Fascism, Them v. Us.

To be sure, Bush's liberal supporters have been disappointed by his efforts. Every newspaper I have listed and many others besides have carried editorials criticizing Bush's policy on imprisonment, his use of torture and above all the sheer ineptitude of the president's war. But here, too, the Cold

War offers a revealing analogy. Like Stalin's Western admirers who, in the wake of Khrushchev's revelations, resented the Soviet dictator not so much for his crimes as for discrediting their Marxism, so intellectual supporters of the Iraq war—among them Michael Ignatieff, Leon Wieseltier, David Remnick, and other prominent figures in the North American liberal establishment—have focused their regrets not on the catastrophic invasion itself (which they all supported) but on its incompetent execution. They are irritated with Bush for giving "preventive war" a bad name.

In a similar vein, those centrist voices that bayed most insistently for blood in the prelude to the Iraq war—the *New York Times* columnist Thomas Friedman demanded that France be voted "Off the Island" (i.e., out of the Security Council) for its presumption in opposing America's drive to war—are today the most confident when asserting their monopoly of insight into world affairs. The same Friedman now sneers at "antiwar activists who haven't thought a whit about the larger struggle we're in" (*New York Times,* 16 August 2006). To be sure, Friedman's Pulitzer-winning pieties are always road-tested for middlebrow political acceptability. But for just that reason they are a sure guide to the mood of the American intellectual mainstream.

Friedman is seconded by Beinart, who concedes that he "didn't realize"(!) how detrimental American actions would be to "the struggle" but insists even so that anyone who won't stand up to "Global Jihad" just isn't a consistent defender of liberal values. Jacob Weisberg, the editor of *Slate,* writing in the *Financial Times,* accuses Democratic critics of the Iraq war of failing "to take the wider, global battle against Islamic fanaticism seriously." The only people qualified to speak on this matter, it would seem, are those who got it wrong initially. ...

In fairness, America's bellicose intellectuals are not alone. In Europe, Adam Michnik, the hero of the Polish intellectual resistance to Communism, has become an outspoken admirer of the embarrassingly Islamophobic Oriana Fallaci; Václav Havel has joined the DC-based Committee on the

Present Danger (a recycled Cold War–era organization dedicated to root-
ing out Communists, now pledged to fighting "the threat posed by global
radical Islamist and fascist terrorist movements"); André Glucksmann in
Paris contributes agitated essays to *Le Figaro* (most recently on 8 August)
lambasting "universal Jihad," Iranian "lust for power," and radical Islam's strategy of "green subversion." All three enthusiastically supported the invasion
of Iraq. . . .

But back home, America's liberal intellectuals are fast becoming a service
class, their opinions determined by their allegiance and calibrated to justify
a political end. In itself this is hardly a new departure: we are all familiar with
intellectuals who speak only on behalf of their country, class, religion, race,
gender or sexual orientation, and who shape their opinions according to
what they take to be the interest of their affinity of birth or predilection.
But the distinctive feature of the liberal intellectual in past times was precisely the striving for universality; not the unworldly or disingenuous denial
of sectional interest but the sustained effort to transcend that interest.

It is thus depressing to read some of the better-known and more
avowedly "liberal" intellectuals in the contemporary USA exploiting their
professional credibility to advance a partisan case. Jean Bethke Elshtain and
Michael Walzer, two senior figures in the country's philosophical establishment (she at the University of Chicago Divinity School, he at the Princeton
Institute), both wrote portentous essays purporting to demonstrate the
justness of necessary wars—she in *Just War Against Terror: The Burden of
American Power in a Violent World,* a preemptive defense of the Iraq War; he
only a few weeks ago in a shameless justification of Israel's bombardments
of Lebanese civilians ("War Fair," *New Republic,* 31 July 2006). In today's
America, neoconservatives generate brutish policies for which liberals provide the ethical fig leaf. There really is no other difference between them.

—Tony Judt[6]

∿

6

The Guilt Weapon

One of the most perverse mechanisms that reinforce the intervention ideology is the constant effort to make critics of recent wars feel guilty. One of the best examples concerns the sad situation of Afghan women. Who is worrying about them today? Who is even trying to find out what is happening to them, especially in the countryside? The same questions could have been asked up until September 2001. But, from the moment the United States decided to wage war against Afghanistan, a "noble" justification had to be found, especially for all those who were not convinced by the "war against terrorism" and had little sympathy for American imperial adventures.

~

War as a Laboratory

The war [in Afghanistan] has been a near-perfect laboratory, according to Michael Vickers, a military analyst at the Center for Strategic and Budgetary Assessments, a defense research center.

Vickers, a former army officer and CIA operative, said the success came because the Qaeda network and the Taliban government sheltering it were overmatched.

"When great powers fight smaller wars," he said, "you can experiment more because there's no doubt you're going to win. You experiment, and there is real feedback. You don't get that very much in the military."

In Afghanistan, Vickers drew a distinction between technical innovation, such as the development of the thermobaric bomb, and what he considers even more important: organizational and tactical innovation, such as linking troops on the ground with bombers in the air.

"This was a new way of war, a new operational concept," Vickers said. "And it was a pretty significant innovation, because we got fairly rapid regime change with it. . . .

"This was the way we planned to overthrow governments."[1]

∾

The horrors inflicted on Afghan women by the Taliban did the trick. Many activists, doubtless with perfect sincerity, suddenly expressed urgent concern over the fate of those women, whereas few people show such concern today. Why? Because everyone is quite aware, then as now, that we are not capable of solving all the world's problems, and especially that such problems as the oppression of women are not solved overnight. But the strength of the propaganda in favor of war is such that even people who are against it feel obliged to express their agreement with the objectives that have been proclaimed in order to justify it, instead of simply denouncing the hypocrisy of the whole maneuver. It seems likely that this sense of obligation stems from the fact that the last thing anti-war activists want to be accused of is "supporting the Taliban." The notion of "support" is in fact at the center of the guilt-trip mechanisms. Let's take a look at it.

∼

The Downing Street Memos: Lucidity and Cynicism

On May 1, 2005, the *Sunday Times* (London) published a "secret and strictly personal" memo for "UK eyes only," summarizing top-level deliberations at the prime minister's office on July 23, 2002, concerning British reaction to the U.S. decision to go to war.[2]

From the July 23, 2002, memo:

> Bush wanted to remove Saddam, through military action, justified by the conjunction of terrorism and WMD. But the intelligence and facts were being fixed around the policy. The NSC [National Security Council] had no patience with the UN route, and no enthusiasm for publishing material on the Iraqi regime's record. There was little discussion in Washington of the aftermath after military action.
>
> The Defence Secretary said that the US had already begun 'spikes of activity' to put pressure on the regime. ...
>
> It seemed clear that Bush had made up his mind to take military action, even if the timing was not yet decided. But the case was thin. Saddam was not threatening his neighbours, and his WMD capability was less than that of Libya, North Korea, or Iran. We should work up a plan for an ultimatum to Saddam to allow back in the UN weapons inspectors. This would also help with the legal justification for the use of force.
>
> The Attorney-General said that the desire for regime change was not a legal base for military action. There were three possible legal bases: self-defence, humanitarian intervention, or UNSC authorization. The first and second could not be the base in this case. Relying on UNSCR 1205 of three years ago would be difficult. The situation might of course change.
>
> The Prime Minister said that it would make a big difference politically and legally if Saddam refused to allow in the UN inspectors.

From another memo, dated July 21, 2002 (point 14):

> It is just possible that an ultimatum could be cast in terms which Saddam would reject (because he is unwilling to accept unfettered

access) and which would not be regarded as unreasonable by the
international community. However, failing that (or an Iraqi attack) we
would be most unlikely to achieve a legal base for military action by
January 2003.

∼

Supporting X

In the run-up to the First World War, a French caricature showed the face
of Jean Jaurès, the socialist leader who strongly opposed the war, merged
with the face of the German Emperor Wilhelm II. Rosa Luxemburg, Karl
Liebknecht, Lenin, Bertrand Russell, Edmund Morel, Eugene Debs—all
those who for one reason or another opposed the wars or the militarism of
their own countries have been accused of "supporting" the enemy.[3] This
method of making opponents of war feel guilty was of course used for the
2003 war against Iraq. The accusation of "anti-Semitism" plays a similar
role in silencing criticism of Israel's treatment of the Palestinian people.

In answer to these reproaches concerning support to the enemy, we
should perhaps start by making the distinction between active (or objective) support and passive (or subjective) support. A state, a movement or an
individual can be said to actively support one side in a conflict when its
actions strengthen the position of that side. On the other hand, passive support, hoping that one side will win, is analogous to the support football fans
give their team while watching a match on television. It is purely sentimental and has no impact on the real world. From an ethical point of view, what
counts is the consequences of our actions, but it can be observed that, like
football fans, many people can argue endlessly over which attitude to adopt
toward certain events—September 11, for example—although that attitude
has no impact on the world.

The antiwar movement unquestionably supported Saddam Hussein, in
the sense of an active support, because, had this movement succeeded in

preventing the war, Saddam would have remained in power (leaving aside that Washington's decision to go to war was made well in advance, at least as early as the summer of 2002, as shown by the "Downing Street memos," and that the antiwar movement had no chance of preventing it). Before considering that as a decisive argument against the movement, thought should be given to some other instances of active support: the British pacifists during the war of 1914–18, who sought a negotiated conclusion to that war, "objectively supported" the German emperor, because such a conclusion would doubtless have allowed him to retain his throne (it might also have allowed Germany to avoid Nazism). During the Second World War, the Anglo-Americans supported Stalin objectively (by arms deliveries, albeit in modest quantities), and in that case, they even supported him subjectively (hoping for his victory over Hitler).

There are many such examples, and thinking about them, one realizes that cases of "objective support" work in all different directions (the protests against the Iraq war also "objectively supported" all who died and are going to die in that war, which is far from over, and who would still be alive without it). The world is much too complicated for us to be able to control all the indirect consequences of our actions. We are faced with a sort of paradox: the only things for which we are morally responsible are the consequences of our actions, but we do not control those consequences, at least not all of them, whereas we perfectly control our "passive support," but that has no direct consequence, at least insofar as it does not inspire us to act and therefore has no moral significance.

The only way out of these dilemmas is not to worry too much about the multitude of objective supports indirectly implied by our actions, but to base these actions on an analysis linking each concrete situation to general principles that can be defended by philosophical and historic reasoning: equality between individuals, whatever the strength of the nations to which they belong, defense of international law as a means of keeping peace, and an anti-imperialist perspective.

Unfortunately, the efforts to neutralize antiwar movements by provoking guilt do not always meet with this sort of response. Rather, it often provokes two kinds of reactions, diametrically opposed, but both of which tend to weaken these movements—what one may call the "neither-nor" stance, and the rhetoric of support.

"Neither-Nor"

This expression refers to slogans often heard in demonstrations against recent wars: "Neither Milosevic nor NATO," "Neither Bush nor Saddam," and, concerning Israel, refers to the practice of condemning in the same breath the policy of Ariel Sharon and that of Hamas and Palestinian suicide bombers. This is obviously a far cry from the slogan heard during the Vietnam War, "The NLF will win!" (shouted then by some of the same individuals who have shifted to the more prudent neither-nor thirty years later). Even if the "support" to the NLF can be dismissed as sentimental rhetoric, to be discussed further on, the current slogans create several false symmetries. First, in all the recent wars, there has been an aggressor and an aggressed; it was neither Iraq nor Yugoslavia that started bombing the United States. To fail to make that distinction, one must have abandoned all notions of national sovereignty and international law.[4] Furthermore, the power and the capacity of the two parties to do harm are not at all comparable. It is the United States and its military power that uphold the extremely unjust world order in which we live. Whatever one may think of the situation in Iraq or in Yugoslavia, it is the United States and not those countries that progressive forces are confronting and will continue to confront in one conflict after another. Every war and every diplomatic success that strengthens the United States should be seen, at least in part, as a setback for most progressive causes.

More important, the neither-nor stance gives the impression that we are somehow situated above it all, outside of time and space, whereas we are living, working, and paying taxes in the aggressor countries or their allies (in contrast, the position "neither Bush nor Saddam" made sense for Iraqis, since they were subjected to both regimes). An elementary moral reaction would be to oppose the aggressions for which our own governments are responsible, or else to approve them outright, before even discussing the responsibility of others.

A frequent argument in favor of the neither-nor position is that it gains respectability, and thus is more effective. This argument is often accompanied by warnings not to repeat the errors of the past, concerning "support" for Stalin or Pol Pot. The "support" for Pol Pot, to the slight extent that it ever existed, was purely subjective, without any influence on the course of events. As for Stalin, note that resistance to Nazism was obviously not based on the slogan "neither Hitler nor Stalin" but more often involved a veritable cult of the Soviet Union and its leader. Whatever one may think retrospectively of that cult, it was massive and its effects (to encourage resistance to Nazism) were by no means all negative.

The argument of effectiveness is thus the easiest to refute: let us simply compare the intensity of the demonstrations against the Vietnam War, when no one was saying "Neither Johnson (or Nixon) nor Ho Chi Minh," with those against the Kosovo war or even the war in Iraq. Indeed, the opposition to the latter is strongest in Muslim countries where everybody, including even Saddam Hussein's worst enemies, acknowledges that the United States is the aggressor and that Iraq is the victim of aggression.

The question of respectability is more delicate to discuss, because it is not clear in whose eyes that respectability is supposed to be established. Either "respectability" means that the position adopted is morally defensible, and the "neither-nor" in no way qualifies, for reasons already mentioned. If, on the other hand, respectability means being acceptable in the eyes of the media and the dominant intellectuals, in that case you may as well recognize that a principled opposition to war will never qualify, and it is self-defeating to entertain any illusions on that score. Then there is public opinion. To be respected by public opinion is certainly a praiseworthy aim, but the job of an antiwar movement is to wage an ideological combat against war propaganda and the mystifications, humanitarian among others, on which it is based. To carry on that combat, shouldn't you start by clarifying your own ideas, and choose slogans that reflect that clarity?

What is most pernicious in the insistence on neither-nor is the idea, widespread even among the most sincere peace advocates, that it is necessary to denounce the adversary—Saddam, Milosevic, Islamic fundamentalists, etc.—to prove that double standards do not apply. Unfortunately, things are not so simple. Nobody can doubt that the caricatures of the German emperor drawn during the First World War were an aspect of war propaganda, which contributed to sending millions of young men to their graves. But few Westerners seem to notice that dehumanizing cartoons of Milosevic or of Mahomet serve the same purpose. The basic principle is nevertheless the same: the things we say and write are heard or read essentially in our own camp, that of the West. Aside from their accuracy, what matters from an ethical viewpoint is the effects they produce here. During wartime, denouncing the crimes of the adversary, even supposing one is accurately informed, which is often not the case, comes down to stimulating the hatred that makes war acceptable.

During the First World War, each side focused on details—some true, others false—to support its claim of defending civilization from barbarism. In retrospect, they seem to have had much in common, and the basic atrocity was the war itself.

All this suggests the need to exercise a certain prudence today in the frequent and virtually automatic denunciations of Islam. We are not (yet) at war with the Muslim world, but the United States (leader of the "free world") is at war in two Muslim countries while threatening Iran and Syria, and, of course, Israel is also seen as part of the "free world." More than the bomb attacks in Madrid and London, this raises the danger of an explosion leading to a more global conflict with the Arab-Muslim world. If that should happen, the current denunciations of Islam can be seen as equivalent to the nationalist propaganda on all sides that preceded the First World War. It is too often forgotten that media campaigns against new "threats" and "enemies" have preceded every major conflagration, often inventing or exaggerating alleged atrocities and acts of barbarism.

~

Denouncing Islam in the Name of Women's Rights: An Old Story

It was principally against the Turks turned Mohametans that our monks wrote so many books, when they could scarcely find another response to the conquerors of Constantinople. Our authors, who are much more numerous than the Janissaries, found it easy to win women over to their side. They persuaded them that Mohamet didn't regard them as intelligent animals, that they were all slaves according to the laws of the Koran, they had no possessions in this world, and that in the next they had no share of paradise.

—Voltaire

~

Another example of the effects produced by the idea that we are above it all: after the Vietnam War, a certain number of American antiwar activists considered that their past opposition to the war gave them a particular responsibility for whatever went wrong afterward, whether the plight of the Vietnamese boat people or the massacres in Cambodia under Pol Pot, and thus a special obligation to denounce those things.[5] That attitude seems to have been most widespread in France, where it contributed heavily to the conversion of the intelligentsia. However, their denunciations did not resound in Indochina but in the West, where they inevitably contributed to the resurgence of imperial ideology. This made it easier for United States leaders to refuse any reparations for the devastation that they had wreaked on Indochina, thereby aggravating the suffering of the peoples of the region, of which the phenomenon of the boat people was in large part a reflection.[6] It also made it easier for them to ideologically prepare for the wars in Central America and in Iraq, which cost hundreds of thousands of lives. But the psychological mechanisms that create a clear conscience are such that hardly any of those who took part in reconstructing the imperial ideology feel any particular responsibility for those crimes.

Still, the main problem for the neither-nor advocates is elsewhere: now that Saddam and Milosevic are in prison or dead, what do they suggest doing with the other half of the neither-nor, Bush or NATO? Certain supporters of humanitarian war in Iraq admit that Bremer's policy was catastrophic, that American companies behaved like vultures, that torture is scandalous, that the destruction of Fallujah is unacceptable and that, of course, it is now their duty to denounce all that.[7] But denouncing and stopping are two very different things, and it is here that the immense gap between the United States and its adversaries shows up again. This gap underscores once more the difference in attitude between human rights defenders who encourage the U.S. armed forces to attack distant countries and, say, the International Brigades fighters during the Spanish Civil War or other real revolutionaries. The point here is not only that the latter risked their lives, contrary to the former, but that they were to a certain extent in control of the force being employed because they were that force. But the human rights defenders have no influence, or at least no moderating influence, on the force they encourage, that is, the U.S. armed forces. Any lucid analysis of American society, as well as of the nature of armies, would indicate that the behavior of the United States in Iraq was perfectly foreseeable, and that is why its armed forces are such a bad instrument for advancing human rights. Despite all their denunciations of Stalinism and their claims to see through abuses of power, the partisans of the right of humanitarian intervention have simply become the "useful idiots" of our time.

～

Salman Rushdie and War

An example of rhetoric justifying imperial wars while putting oneself on the high moral ground is provided by Salman Rushdie. In a 2002 article defending his support for the war in Afghanistan, he suggested that the United States put Ahmed Chalabi in power in Iraq after overthrowing Saddam Hussein rather than installing a new military power: "I can't speak for the others, but my own view is pretty straightforward. If America gets into bed with scumbags, it loses the moral high ground, and once that ground is lost, the argument is lost with it."[8] Given that it would scarcely be a novelty for America to "get into bed with scumbags," what should be done if it happens again? Rushdie proposes appealing to public opinion. But with the public's "patriotism" and indifference, both cultivated by the media, this is not very realistic, to say the least. Does American public opinion care about the fate of the Serbs in Kosovo or the situation in the Afghan countryside? Who in the American population was going to protest against Chalabi's installation (if the Americans followed Rushdie's advice) in the face of his extreme unpopularity in Iraq, where many people considered him to be precisely a "scumbag"? When American soldiers are killed, as in Iraq, public opinion begins to take notice, but one can scarcely suppose that the advocates of humanitarian war count on large numbers of U.S. soldiers getting killed in order to exert their own moral influence.

∾

The neither-nor approach is also symptomatic of a more general trend on the left, after the failure of communism, toward a quasi-religious position of moral absolutism. The discourse of the left, especially the far left in France, today often comes down to a catalogue of good intentions (open borders and guaranteed full employment) that are not accompanied by any political strategy to accomplish these goals. One is reminded of the words of Jesus, "My kingdom is not of this world." The failure of "scientific socialism" has given way to a return to utopian socialism. This tendency is often accompanied by adoption of an irritating moral posturing: neither this nor that, but no concrete alternative in the real world. Obviously, doing nothing that could have any impact on reality carries no risk, and there is no need to worry about being accused of supporting Stalin or Pol Pot.

But, at that point, why continue to claim to be engaged in political action? This attitude of effortless moral purity is typical of a philosophical or religious aversion to the real world, which is the exact opposite of politics. Proposing a way out of this impasse is far beyond the scope of this book. It can nevertheless be recalled that all effective politics has its dark side and its drawbacks and that politics often comes down to defending the lesser evil, such as international law rather than American hegemony, which religious absolutism tends to refuse to do. A symptom of this moral purism is the general reluctance of the French left to recognize that President Jacques Chirac, whatever his other shortcomings, by refusing to go along with the United States aggression in Iraq, took a historic decision that could do much more to preserve peace between Europe and the Arab world than countless expressions of good intentions.

The Rhetoric of "Support"

Finally, a few words should be said about the rhetoric of "support" to revolutionary causes and liberation movements in the Third World, rhetoric quite prevalent within the small minority in the West that takes anti-imperialist positions and which is the exact opposite of the neither-nor, though with certain drawbacks of its own. "We" are supposed to support the Palestinian or Iraqi resistance, or Chávez, or, at one time or another in the past, the Soviet Union, China, Cuba, Vietnam, etc.

What follows is in no way a criticism of those militants who are concretely engaged alongside revolutionary struggles and who, as a result, go beyond the stage of rhetoric, but rather concerns the debates that take place in the West and the splits they create. A large part of the disputes within the far left, between "Stalinists" and "Trotskyists," for example, concerning support of this or that faction, suffer because the support being discussed is not clearly defined, and, in particular, the distinction between active and passive support is ignored. Most of us have neither weapons nor secrets to hand over to a cause with which we sympathize. Our "support" is at best sentimental and it is hard to see why we should behave like supporters of football teams. If all-out interventionism is largely a residue of the colonial mentality, the rhetoric of support can be considered an indirect heritage of the Third International, even if it has often been outdone in that particular exercise by various Trotskyist groups. The Communist International was a powerful and relatively centralized movement. It meant something when it supported, through obedient parties, such and such a movement or struggle in a given country, which does not mean that the method chosen was necessarily effective or appropriate, but simply that it had real political effects. That period, however, belongs to the past, and it is of no use to continue to act as though there exists somewhere a revolutionary headquarters that is going to listen to us and pass along our enlightened opinions to the other ends of the earth.

The rhetoric of support has numerous drawbacks. It locks militants into useless discussions regarding conflicts over which they have not the slightest influence (what should Trotsky have done in 1924?) and isolates them from the general population, which quite rightly regards such discussions as modern counterparts of the Byzantine dispute over the sex of angels. Moreover, it leads them into a pursuit of historical erudition that gets in the way of understanding today's world or persuading other people they need to change it. Finally, those imaginary supports end up being followed by often painful and politically catastrophic disillusion. How many people have reproached themselves for having "supported" Stalin, Mao, or Pol Pot, and subsequently abandoned all political activity, when, unless they actually lived and were active in the Soviet Union, China, or Cambodia, all they ever really did was to express opinions, perhaps mistaken, but with no impact on the course of world events?

The latest avatar of the support problem concerns the Iraqi resistance. How does one dare support those cutthroats and adversaries of democracy? To which others reply: Don't peoples have the right to defend themselves? Note first of all that when the USSR invaded Afghanistan, the Western consensus demanding their withdrawal did not usually dwell on its support to the Afghan resistance, support which would have raised serious questions if the nature of that resistance had come under closer scrutiny. It was enough to consider that it was necessary to put a stop to an illegal invasion. The same can be said for a number of other invasions, that of Kuwait by Iraq, for example. The pretexts furnished by the United States to invade Iraq were, if anything, even more far-fetched, and certainly do not justify suspension of opposition to invasion, without ever raising the question of support.

One of the main things wrong with the rhetoric of support is that it accepts the logic of the adversary: they accuse us of "supporting" the other camp. Instead of justifying that support, it is better to answer that what we do is no different from what they do in similar circumstances.

Moreover, a minimum of modesty should lead us to think that, far from us supporting a resistance that isn't asking for anything, it is the resistance that supports us. After all, the resistance is much more effective in blocking the U.S. military machine, at least for a while, than the millions of demonstrators who marched peacefully against the war and who unfortunately did not manage to stop the soldiers or the bombs. Without the Iraqi resistance, the United States would perhaps today be attacking Damascus, Teheran, Caracas, or Havana. If I do not claim to "support" the Iraqi resistance, for which I am sometimes criticized, the reason, among other things, is that an Iraqi insurgent could always ask, echoing Stalin's remark about the pope, how many divisions will you send into battle?[9]

It is true, as is often pointed out in response to Stalin's wisecrack, that ideas can be effective. And the combat on the level of ideas, for example, through opinion tribunals such as the World Tribunal on Iraq and its branch, the Brussels Tribunal, can be considered a "support" to the Iraqi resistance (and be denounced or applauded as such). But they can also be seen as fitting into a much broader perspective, which will be sketched in the following pages.

~

The British Press Prior to the Resistance, or, Dizzy with Success

For a political leader, few therapies compare with military victory. For a leader who went to war in the absence of a single political ally who believed in the war as unreservedly as he did, Iraq now looks like vindication on an astounding scale.

—Hugo Young, *The Guardian*, April 15, 2003

There's no doubt that the desire to bring good, to bring American values to the rest of the world, and especially now to the Middle East ... is now increasingly tied up with military power.

—BBC1, "Panorama," April 13, 2003

They've covered his face in the Stars and Stripes! This gets better by the minute ... ha ha, better by the minute.

—ITV, *Tonight with Trevor McDonald*, April 11, 2003

Yes, too many people died in the war. Too many people always die in war. War is nasty and brutish, but at least this conflict was mercifully short. The death toll has been nothing like as high as had been widely feared. Thousands have died in this war, millions have died at the hands of Saddam. ... In the mind of Tony Blair, I don't think this war was ever wholly, or even mainly, about any threat posed by Saddam. These were arguments designed to make the conflict accord with international law. The Prime Minister was never very convincing that Saddam was a real and present danger. ... For Mr. Blair, getting rid of Saddam is legitimacy enough.

—Andrew Rawnsley, "The Voices of Doom Were So Wrong,"
The Observer, April 13, 2003

No one can deny that victory happened. The existential fact sweeps aside the prior agonising. ... We got rid of a pitiless enemy of humanity. What more do you want? All that agonising about the whys and wherefores? Forget it.

—Hugo Young, *The Guardian*, April 15, 2003

Bush as Radical Liberal Revolutionary

The great irony is that the Baathists and Arab dictators are opposing the U.S. in Iraq because—unlike many leftists—they understand exactly what this war is about. They understand that U.S. power is not being used in Iraq for oil, or imperialism, or to shore up a corrupt status quo, as it was in Vietnam and elsewhere in the Arab world during the Cold War. They understand that this is the most radical-liberal revolutionary war the U.S. has ever launched—a war of choice to install some democracy in the heart of the Arab-Muslim world.

—Thomas L. Friedman[10]

~

7

Prospects, Dangers and Hopes

Even if we accept that the advocates of humanitarian intervention have no satisfactory response to a whole series of questions—What is the nature of the agent supposed to intervene? What reason is there to trust his sincerity? What replaces international law? How can intervention be reconciled with democracy?—the eternal question remains: What should we do?

I do not claim to have a satisfactory answer. Indeed, it is by no means easy to get out of the state of war in which we find ourselves. Moreover, to do so would require radical changes in the Western mindset, including in progressive circles. To start with, let's look at what needs to be changed in our overall vision of how we relate to the rest of the world. Next let us consider what should be the priorities of peace movements, the information battle and, finally, the reasons for hope.

Another Vision of the World Is Possible

What I have written up to now is by no means intended as a plea for staying home and "minding our own business." It is completely possible to find ways to act while taking into account global factors (the state of the world,

the reality of North-South relations, etc.), the relationship of forces that condition our acts, and the place where they occur. But we should start by aban-
doning the pretense of being able to solve every problem on earth. Colonialism, like the Third International, belongs to the past. And this implies we
should not feel responsible for everything that happens.

On the other hand, there are a number of things we can do that do not
require any intervention, regarding matters for which we ought to feel
responsible but seem of concern to relatively few people. First of all, there is
the whole economic aspect of North-South relations: debt, the prices of raw
materials, access to cheap medicines. If we have so much money to spend on
"humanitarian wars," then why isn't there enough for actions whose humanitarian character would be unequivocal? Why do the people who demand
that we all feel guilty for not having intervened militarily in Rwanda, where
about 8,000 people died every day for a hundred days, not feel responsible
that the same number of people die in Africa every day, all year-round, of dis-
eases that are relatively easy to cure? The examples of Cuba or the Indian
state of Kerala show that public health can reach a high level in relatively
poor countries. Therefore one cannot say that people die from poverty
alone. As for the cost, the "war for democracy" in Iraq costs much more than
what would be needed to save thousands of lives every day.

There is a world of difference between intervention and cooperation.
Unlike intervention, cooperation is carried out with the agreement of the
host government. Few governments in the Third World reject cooperation
if it is sincere. With so much misery in the world it is hard to imagine a situation in which, for a given expenditure of money and effort, cooperation
would not save more human lives than intervention. Even the extreme
example of Rwanda does not refute that suggestion.

It follows that, contrary to what some may think, there is no conflict
between strict respect for national sovereignty and a (non-hypocritical)
defense of human rights. It would be enough to allocate to cooperation the
resources we claim ready for altruistic intervention.

Furthermore, there is need for a "cultural revolution" in our relations to "the others"—a bit more modesty and less arrogance. Culinary, musical, or artistic traditions from the Third World have become more and more popular and appreciated in recent decades. But what is missing in the West is any serious attempt at political understanding of the countries of the South, including their movements and leaders. First , there is the problem of information. As soon as our media tell us that atrocities have been committed by a leader or political movement of the South, most of our Western progressives accept the story without question. Now, if the lies about the links between Iraq and al-Qaeda or about Iraq weapons of mass destruction are relatively well-known, other systematic features of war propaganda, for example, what was really going on in Kosovo before the NATO bombing or the history of relations between Israelis and Palestinians, deserve to be better known and understood. A grasp of such past events ought to inspire a reasonable skepticism about future media allegations used to justify going to war.

In particular, the Kosovo war was the culmination of a decade of media bombardment in favor of "humanitarian intervention," which was supposed to free us from the notion of national sovereignty and, more generally, of international law. The advocates of that intervention zealously spread every bit of one-sided propaganda for war, whether originating with local protagonists seeking to get NATO to fight for their side, or used by the United States to inaugurate a series of post–Cold War "humanitarian" wars.

The result was a Manichean vision of the Yugoslav conflicts, with Milosevic as principal villain. In this context, Western media and publics accepted without hesitation the idea that the ultimatum thrown at the Serbs at Rambouillet was the result of "negotiations," which broke down solely due to the bad faith of the president of the country to be bombed, and that the combats between government forces and armed Albanian rebels (secretly aided by the United States and Germany) were "ethnic cleansing." A war waged to oblige the Yugoslav president to deliver his country over to NATO occupation became, as the bombs fell, a war against a "genocide" invented by NATO war propaganda.[1] By the time the war was over, and no traces of genocide were found, the public had lost interest. The subsequent "ethnic cleansing" of non-Albanians from Kosovo has been largely ignored by the media, or dismissed as understandable "revenge."

~

The Crimes of Saddam Hussein

Downing Street has admitted to *The Observer* that repeated claims by Tony Blair that "400,000 bodies had been found in Iraqi mass graves" is untrue, and only about 5,000 corpses have so far been uncovered.

The claims by Blair in November and December of last year, were given widespread credence, quoted by MPs and widely published, including in the introduction to a US government pamphlet on Iraq's mass graves. In that publication—"Iraq's Legacy of Terror: Mass Graves" produced by USAID, the US government aid distribution agency—Blair is quoted from 20 November last year: "We've already discovered, just so far, the remains of 400,000 people in mass graves."

On 14 December Blair repeated the claim in a statement issued by Downing Street in response to the arrest of Saddam Hussein and posted on the Labour Party website that: "The remains of 400,000 human beings [have] already [been] found in mass graves."

The USAID website, which quotes Blair's 400,000 assertion, states: "If these numbers prove accurate, they represent a crime against humanity surpassed only by the Rwandan genocide of 1994, Pol Pot's Cambodian killing fields in the 1970s, and the Nazi Holocaust of World War II."[2]

These citations from *The Observer* illustrate the way the Western propaganda system works. An assertion that is purely factual ("the remains of 400,000 human beings have already been found") but false (and deliberately so, since the people who make it are the very ones who order the exhumations in the mass graves) is launched by a government and repeated on a large scale (by the British Labor Party, a U.S. news agency, etc.). It is indeed corrected, but only once, and without any echo of that rectification in foreign countries, notably the United States. So the lie remains in the public consciousness and has its effect: if someone points out that the U.S. war has cost the lives of 100,000 Iraqi civilians, the immediate answer is: "Ah, yes, but they found 400,000 bodies in Saddam's mass graves."

Furthermore, this sort of confession ought to encourage skepticism toward other government assertions. It rarely works this way.

Instead, a frequent reaction is to say that this type of disinformation doesn't really matter, because, in any case, "Saddam is a brutal dictator." But this is not the point. What would be the reaction if the leader of a Third World country multiplied by a factor of 80 the number of dead at Sabra and Chatila (160,000), or during the Vietnam War (240 million) or in the invasion of Iraq (8 million)? How much credibility would he retain?

∽

We must stop being afraid of direct contact with the other side. How many of us wanted to hear the opinion of ordinary Arab citizens during the first Gulf war? Or even the second? How many were willing to listen to the viewpoint of Serbs or Greeks during the Kosovo war? How many are ready today to discuss the Iraq war openly and frankly with intellectuals described as "Islamists"? Why was it necessary to wait for the work of a new school of Israeli historians before taking into consideration things that everyone in the Arab world knows about (what happened in Palestine in 1948)? Doesn't genuine internationalism consist of challenging our own feeling of moral (and not only cultural) superiority and listening to and discussing events with those who are under constant attack from our media and governments? Will the global justice movement succeed in establishing channels permitting direct discussions between populations, channels that would replace the odd form of "solidarity" that consists today in calling on Western governments to intervene even more than they are already willing to do in the internal affairs of other countries?

The surprising fact that the AFL-CIO went against all its history to take a critical position toward U.S. foreign policy by calling for withdrawal of troops from Iraq may have something to do with the Iraqi trade unionists who came to talk with their American colleagues to describe to them face-to-face the real situation in their country. It is probably by organizing such direct exchanges, especially between peace movements, that public opinion in the United States and Britain can be radically changed.[3] But this sort of communication requires that Western governments agree to issue the necessary visas.[4]

This brings us to the most striking illustration of what must be changed: we are mentally very far from Iraq—much more so than we were "Far from Vietnam" when several French directors made a film with that title in 1967. Fallujah was a Guernica with no Picasso. A city of 300,000 was deprived of water, electricity, and food, emptied of most of its inhabitants who ended up parked in camps. Then came the methodical bombing and recapture of the city, block by block. When soldiers occupied a hospital, the *New York Times* managed to justify this act on grounds that the hospital served as an enemy propaganda center by exaggerating the number of casualties.[5] And by the way, just how many casualties were there? Nobody knows, there is no body count for Iraqis. When estimates are published, even by reputable scientific reviews, they are denounced as exaggerated. Finally, the inhabitants were allowed to return to their devastated city, by way of military checkpoints, and start to sift through the rubble, under the watchful eye of soldiers and biometric controls.

~

Leftist Legitimization of the Occupation

The occupying powers, well aware of an international media presence, will never commit the same crimes that his regime did. Despite arbitrary arrests, cases of torture condemned by Amnesty International and restrictions on the press, it is hard to equate the abuses of the occupation with the brutal conduct of an army on full battle alert. ...

So the slow progress of the occupying forces has a disproportionate impact.

But their many mistakes—some of which have been very dramatic, like the disbanding of the army—have subtler repercussions. Important religious dignitaries have been arrested, as have eminent tribal leaders. The blunders continue. Occasionally car passengers are crushed by an armored vehicle, but nothing seems to trigger revolt or even demonstrations of more than a few thousand.[6]

The article was published before the revelations on Abu Ghraib and the attack on Fallujah, but the peremptory tone ("never") reflects perfectly Western certitudes as to our benevolence in comparison to others.

～

In response to all that, how many protests were there? How many demonstrations in front of U.S. embassies? How many petitions in allied countries to call on the government to demand that the United States stop? Which aid organizations are concerned with those victims as much as with those of Hurricane Katrina? How many newspaper editorials denounce those crimes?

Who are the champions of "civil society" and nonviolence who stop to recall that the tragedy of Fallujah began when, shortly after the invasion, its inhabitants demonstrated peacefully and the Americans fired into the crowd, killing sixteen people? And there is not just Fallujah. There is also Najaf, Al Kaïm, Haditha, Samarra, Bakouba, Hit, Bouhriz, Tal Afar.

The Brussels Tribunal frequently receives reports of disappearances and assassinations in Iraq. Not of Islamic fanatics or evil Saddamists, but of intellectuals just as "Western" as those in the West who come up with excuses (Saddam, Islam) to ignore their fate. The "Salvador option" is well under way in Iraq.[7] But to whom should we pass on these reports? Who cares?

We are more or less back to the situation that prevailed at the start of the Vietnam War, between 1962 and 1967, when to show concern for the fate of Vietnamese peasants bombed and burned by the U.S. Air Force was perceived by the American liberal intelligentsia as a sign of being "soft on communism." Today, "Islamists" have taken the place of communists. A big difference is that in those days there existed, outside the United States, a relatively strong communist movement (including its competing Maoist and Trotskyist branches) which to a certain extent was able to contradict the dominant discourse. Today, however, the American liberal ideology has conquered the entire Western world, including for the most part whatever remains of the communist parties.

~

Strategists Have Ideas

Strikes at population targets (per se) are likely not only to create a counterproductive wave of revulsion abroad and at home, but greatly increase the risk of enlarging the war with China and the Soviet Union. Destruction of locks and dams, however—if handled right—might (perhaps after the next pause) offer promise. It should be studied. Such destruction does not kill or drown people. By shallow-flooding the rice, it leads after time to widespread starvation (more than a million?) unless food is provided— which we could offer to do "at the conference table."[8]

~

What do the NGOs have to say about all this, especially the human rights defenders? As the Canadian professor of international law Michael Mandel rightly remarks, at the start of the war, Human Rights Watch, Amnesty International, and other groups issued a firm appeal to the "belligerents" (as neutral a term as possible) to respect the rules of war. But not a word was said about the illegality of the war itself, about what international law considers the "supreme crime" committed by those who started the war.[9] These organizations are in the position of those who recommend that rapists use condoms. That may seem better than nothing, but finally, given the relationship of forces, even the condoms won't be used. The ideology of intervention in the name of human rights has been the perfect instrument to destroy peace movements and anti-imperialist movements. But once that intervention takes place on a large scale, human rights and the Geneva Conventions are massively violated.

~

Amnesty International and the Iraqi Constitution

In 2005, the Brussels Tribunal received a letter written by a human rights activist in Baghdad in reaction to an Amnesty International campaign in favor of an Iraqi constitution based on human rights. This letter explains why asking that the constitution respect human rights, under the current circumstances, comes down to legitimizing the occupation. This is a political choice, but it is not explicitly recognized as such by Amnesty International:

I hear Amnesty International is campaigning for Human Rights in the new Iraqi draft constitution. How wonderful that they are concerned about our human rights in the future ... but what about now? Why doesn't Amnesty International campaign or at least say something about the hundreds of thousands of innocent Iraqis who are held for months, years in the American prisons, without the least rights? The known and the unknown prisons inside and outside Iraq? Why don't they do something about the hundreds of Iraqis, whose bodies are found every day on the garbage piles, with evidences of horrible torture on their bodies after they had been disappeared for a few days? What about the miserable life the Iraqi government is giving the Iraqis for months now, in every field? Does Amnesty International consider the rewriting of the constitution now a legal process? Obviously it does, but on what bases? The war and occupation of Iraq are illegal (even Kofi Annan said it). Who wrote the draft? A member of the writing committee admitted that a draft was sent from the US. So, how far is this legal?

I would like to ask Amnesty International one question: why is it so necessary to write a new constitution for Iraq now? All the political parties, the government, the National Assembly, the media etc. are preoccupied with the [controversial points] in the constitution for months now, and will be for the next few months. Meanwhile, the country is full of problems: the security, the services, the economy, the environment, the corruption, the Human Rights conduct of the Iraqi government ... to mention only few. ... Two days ago I went to a dentist compound, one of the biggest in Baghdad, where at least 50 dentists work. They could not pull out my tooth because they did not have anesthetic ... a very common problem in the Iraqi hospitals for months. Too bad for my teeth, but imagine with emergency cases?

In Tal Afar families did not get the food ration, neither any other food since the beginning of this year. In many Iraqi towns, the majority, there is no authority, no law, no police, no courts, only the armed militias and their political parties. Racial cleansing has begun in many parts of Iraq. The government in the heavily fortified Green Zone is very busy working on the constitution.

During the last attack on Haditha, for more than two weeks, all the news programs, the dialogue, the forums were focused on the constitution and in the meantime an Iraqi major city was practically slaughtered. No one said a word about it as if it was happening on the moon. Do you think that this is just a coincidence? And, by the way, it happened and is happening continuously in other places.

There are so many problems in Iraq now, so many crimes committed daily, where innocent people are killed, arrested, tortured ... Why is it so important to neglect all these crimes and be busy with the constitution? Why is it so urgent?

Saddam did not write the Iraqi constitution, and if there were some changes or resolutions added to it during the last 30 years, they can be canceled, simple. We can keep our constitution until we have a proper government and national assembly. After we are done with the most urgent problems, we can take our time writing the most humanitarian and progressive constitution in the world!

Maybe more dangerous is the fact that rewriting the constitution now is deepening the divisions between the Iraqis and pushing them to the verge of civil war, because some of them were given guarantees to participate in the political process, which they refused in the beginning, and after they agreed, the guarantees proved to be untrue. Now these groups are saying that they were deceived, and they reject the draft presented to the National Assembly. All these problems are for what? Just to help Bush look more successful in Iraq, to give him more diplomatic credit?

To hold the election, thousands were killed and Fallujah demolished. Now, what is needed to impose a constitution? A civil war?

Can't you see that it is a game? The political parties and ethnic, sectarian groups are taking the chance of imposing a constitution convenient to their interests and their masters', not the interests of Iraq. I am not saying this out of my own prejudice, no, they admit it themselves, openly. Also, there is a very unhealthy, nonobjective atmosphere in which this constitution is written, which is something expected and normal in the current situation. But it is not the right way to write a constitution.

I know very well who are the friends and the enemies of Iraq and its people. I have nothing against any international organization. On the contrary, I, personally, am badly in need of an international organization that can help me in my campaign on the Missing. I want these organizations to come here and work on the violations that the occupation did and is doing in Iraq. We need them badly to see what the occupation is covering by rewriting the constitution.

—Sabah Ali[10]

Finally, what is it that anti-war movements ought to do? Before answering that question, another problem should be raised, concerning the real position of those movements within the overall political balance of forces.

Getting Away from Idealism

The word *idealism* can have several meanings. Here what is meant is an expression of good intentions that is not accompanied by an adequate analysis of the relationship of forces in general, and in particular, the position occupied within that relationship of forces by the person expressing those good intentions. Unfortunately, idealism in this sense causes considerable confusion in progressive circles. The feeling of responsibility for things over which one has no control sometimes leads totally powerless opponents of the war to identify with United States power to the extent of trying to figure out "what we should do" to fix the mess it has made, instead of simply demanding that it withdraw its troops.

Such worries reflect the failure to explicitly formulate a couple of key questions, which tend to be implicitly answered without ever being discussed. Does the United States have the right, the ability. or even the duty to prevent civil war in Iraq? And do movements opposed to the war have the obligation to propose alternative solutions to the Iraqi disaster?

Let's start with the first question.

As for the right, we are back to the matter of international law. Once you accept that any country can intervene in the internal affairs of another where it figures that a danger of civil war exists, we will soon get to the state of war of all against all. And if we consider that the invasion of Iraq was illegitimate, then evoking the risk of civil war to justify the occupation makes no more sense than justifying the Soviet occupation of Afghanistan.

As to the question of ability, there is a certain tendency on the idealistic left to oppose war because it is immoral, even if the United States is able to win easily. Noam Chomsky illustrates that point of view, combining a strong moral disapproval with an extreme overestimation of American power, when he declares:

> What about Iraq? Well, I must say it is a very surprising result what has happened. It should have been one of the easier military occupations in history. First of all I thought the war itself would be over in two days and then that the occupation would immediately succeed. ... My guess is the MIT electrical engineering department could have had the energy system running in Iraq by now. It's hard to imagine that degree of incompetence and failure and it is partly because of the way they are treating people. They have been treating people in such a way that engenders resistance and hatred and fear. But I still find it hard to imagine that they can't crush guerrilla-style resistance.[11]

This leaves aside, however, the extent to which American society is permeated with racism, ignorance, and arrogance; that the MIT engineers, who in principle are doubtless equally capable of reinforcing the dikes in New Orleans, are only a tiny minority of that society; that they are not necessarily eager to go to work in Iraq; and that the Iraqi resistance is not only the result of the hatred provoked by the occupation, but has been carefully prepared by the former regime.

Both the current management of the occupation and that of the New Orleans hurricane disaster suggest that the United States is far from being all-powerful. The possession of advanced technology enabling no-risk long-range bombing is so far not, fortunately, the key to world domination. Even if the comparison may not please everybody, the Muslim-Arab world that is massively opposed to the U.S. occupation of Iraq momentarily finds itself in the position of David against Goliath, but as is apparent, the victory of Goliath is not assured.

~

Elementary, My Dear Watson

The lamest defense I could offer—one used by many supporters of the war as they slam into reverse gear—is that I still support the principle of invasion, it's just the Bush administration screwed it up. But as one antiwar friend snapped at me when I mooted this argument, "Yeah, who would ever have thought that supporting George Bush in the illegal invasion of an Arab country would go wrong?" She's right: the truth is that there was no pure Platonic ideal of The Perfect Invasion to support, no abstract idea we lent our names to. There was only Bush, with his cluster bombs, depleted uranium, IMF-ed up economic model, bogus rationale and unmistakable stench of petrol, offering his war, his way. (Expecting Tony Blair to use his influence was, it is now clear, a delusion, as he refuses to even frontally condemn the American torture camp at Guantánamo Bay.)

The evidence should have been clear to me all along: the Bush administration would produce disaster. Let's look at the major mistakes-cum-crimes. Who would have thought they would unleash widespread torture, with over 10,000 people disappearing without trial into Iraq's secret prisons? Anybody who followed the record of the very same people—from Rumsfeld to Negroponte—in Central America in the 1980s. Who would have thought they would use chemical weapons? Anybody who looked up Bush's stance on chemical weapons treaties (he uses them for toilet paper) or checked Rumsfeld's record of flogging them to tyrants. Who would have thought they would impose shock therapy mass privatization on the Iraqi economy, sending unemployment soaring to 60 percent—a guarantee of ethnic strife? Anybody who followed the record of the US toward Russia, Argentina, and East Asia. Who could have known that they would cancel all reconstruction funds, when electricity and water supplies are still below even Saddam's standards? Anybody who looked at their domestic policies.

—Johann Hari[12]

~

As for duty, some time ago, an American friend wrote me regarding the situation in Iraq: "What needs to be done now is a different question from knowing whether to support the war in the beginning. Now that the harm has been done, nobody knows how to repair all the damage. Leaving American troops in Iraq indefinitely is obviously not a good idea (from a progressive point of view), but it is not easy to know what would be a better alternative. Even in the peace movement, people are afraid that a simple American withdrawal, with nothing to put in its place, would lead to civil war."

Well, the Americans have stayed on since then, and the country sinks ever closer to civil war. Finally, the question as to whether the Americans have a duty to stabilize the situation in Iraq is the easiest of all. Inasmuch as it is manifestly impossible for them to do so, what sense does it make to hope that by staying on they will repair the damage they have caused in Iraq? Moreover, experience in Iraq and elsewhere shows that foreign intervention tends to provoke internal conflict, even civil war, as the occupying power seeks to gain support by favoring one group or faction against others.

～

The Democratic Opposition

Having the strongest military in the world is the first step, but we also have to have a strong commitment to using our military in smart ways that further peace, stability, and security around the world.

—Hillary Rodham Clinton

Force will be used without asking anyone's permission when circumstances warrant.

—Joseph Biden, now chairman of the
Senate Foreign Relations Committee[13]

Richard Holbrooke, who's been dubbed the "closest thing the party has to a Kissinger" by one foreign policy analyst, even tacked to Bush's right, arguing in February 2003 that anything less than an invasion of Iraq would undermine international law.[14]

～

Let's ask the second question: Is it up to the antiwar movement to propose solutions to the dramatic situation in Iraq? A positive response is not so simple, because one needs to know the real role that could be played by such "solutions." What characterizes idealism in politics is to act as if the world is full of well-meaning folk, sitting around a table trying to work out an intellectually complicated problem. Whereas political problems are generally not intellectually complicated. Take the example of Palestine: one could demand the application of all the United Nations resolutions, which would doubtless be the fairest solution, and in any case would not demand any particular intellectual exertion. Of course, it's impossible to achieve, and the reason is the relationship of forces—which is where the real problem lies.

People without political power who propose "peace plans," such as the Geneva agreement on Palestine, rarely ask themselves how to establish a balance of forces that would allow their plans to be adopted. Worse still, proposing such plans in a vacuum, that is, without the support of an effective political power, and letting the media report on it as they please, can have a demobilizing effect, giving public opinion the impression that the problem is in the process of being solved, an effect that gets in the way of any favorable solution.

In the case of Iraq, any "proposal" that could be made by the opposition movements, for example, a replacement of U.S. troops by those of the United Nations, or any other form of internationalization of the war, would have the same drawback as the "peace plans" in the style of the Geneva agreement on Palestine. Having no means to impose the proposed solutions, however brilliant they might be, the simple act of proposing them would be a subtle form of aid to the occupation—focusing on the intellectual search for solutions, rather than building a mass movement to put pressure on the U.S. government to get out.

The purpose of peace movements cannot be to provide such aid, on the pretext that this would be the best solution for the Iraqis. It is true that nobody knows what would happen if the Americans left Iraq. But nobody knows what state Iraq will be in if they leave in ten or twenty years. In any case, it is hard to see how they can stay there indefinitely—the French stayed 130 years in Algeria, the Belgians 80 years in the Congo, the Americans a dozen years in Vietnam, and the Israelis 20 years in Lebanon. But in the end, they were all chased out.

The idea of "proposing solutions" is also the reflection inside opposition movements of a confidence in the almighty power of the West, with the slight difference that these movements consider themselves much more intelligent than the Bush administration. It would be far more realistic to admit that we do not have solutions to other people's problems, and this being the case, we would do better not to interfere in their affairs.

In contrast to the idealistic tendencies on the left, there are people, call them conservatives, who are worried about the budget deficits deepened by the war, worried about the hatred aroused by U.S. policy, worried about the demoralization of the troops, worried about loss of American lives.[15] Worried also about the domestic situation: social polarization, poor education, massive outsourcing and sale of enterprises to foreigners, disappearance of public services, growing concentration of media leading to uniform presentation of information, and so on. For all those reasons, that part of the population would like to "cultivate its own garden" and see the U.S. government tend to the well-being of its own population instead of "building democracy in Iraq." Of course, it is in that part of the population that we hear annoying arguments such as: "Let's go home, we have tried everything to bring them democracy." As if invading a country and killing tens of thousands of its inhabitants, while displaying typically colonial attitudes and practices, was an appropriate way to establish democracy.

Nevertheless, if the conflict in Iraq goes on, or if other countries are attacked, there will have to be an alliance, or at least an objective, between the left and that part of the conservative right. Moreover, the forces that those two groups are confronting—that is, the neoconservatives who dominate the Republican Party and the humanitarian imperialists who dominate the Democratic Party, the Zionists who are influential in both parties, and various military-industrial lobbies—are more formidable than the forces they can mobilize even if they unite.

We can expect to see in coming years that part of the political debate will be centered on the issue of imperialism, intervention, relations with the Muslim world, and that the battle lines on these essential issues will not correspond to the traditional left-right cleavage. The interventionist "center" will attempt to dismiss its critics with the habitual niceties, calling them "extremists," "totalitarians," "anti-Semites," etc., but that will not silence the debate.

The attitude that should be adopted by peace movements is to situate themselves realistically within a global perspective. Indeed, they cannot guarantee a happy outcome to the conflict in Iraq—because that is something nobody can do. Nor could the British anticolonialists guarantee that the end of the Raj would not have tragic consequences. Would that have been a reason it insist that England occupy India indefinitely? On the other hand, those movements are able to struggle within Western societies to get them to adopt a radically different attitude toward the Third World, an attitude based roughly on the demands of the countries of the South for peaceful cooperation, nonintervention, respect for national sovereignty and conflict resolution using the United Nations as intermediary. Withdrawal from Iraq would be a first step in that direction.

~

Cutting and Running?

Out of the black smoke and ashes of that terrible day, America stood up strong, united, and determined. After careful deliberation, we answered back. We toppled the Taliban in Afghanistan, where al-Qaeda had trained.

—Senator Bill Frist, press release: "Frist Denounces Democrats' Plan to Cut and Run," June 30, 2006

U.S. Senate Majority Leader Bill Frist said Monday that the Afghan guerrilla war can never be won militarily and called for efforts to bring the Taliban and their supporters into the Afghan government. The Tennessee Republican said he had learned from briefings that Taliban fighters were too numerous and had too much popular support to be defeated by military means.

—Associated Press, "U.S. Senate Majority Leader Calls for Efforts to Bring Taliban into Afghan Government," October 2, 2006[16]

∿

There is no reason to believe that those demands are any more utopian than the idea of world stability under American hegemony, nor that, had we followed such a policy systematically for the last half-century, human rights would not be better respected than they are now.

Let us consider now one of the first areas where the combat for such an alternative policy must be carried on: the area of information, or, more generally, our representation of the world.

Imperialism Watch

In recent decades, there has been a proliferation of organizations, essentially based in rich countries, watching and denouncing violations of human rights in poor countries. Whenever I happen to discuss with representatives of these organizations why they do not denounce military aggressions, for example in Iraq, the answer is roughly that this is not their field and that they can't do everything. They are concerned with human rights, period. That response would be defensible if the discourse of these organizations had not become hegemonic to a point that scarcely any other viewpoint, for example the defense of national sovereignty, can get a hearing. Moreover, they push their own priority to the point of being strictly neutral concerning aggressive wars, while denouncing the violations of human rights brought about by those wars—that is, they act as if there were no necessary link between the two. After all, those organizations do not refrain from denouncing those who are responsible for violating human rights—why then not include in that denunciation those who start wars?

~

Human Rights Watch and War

"To preserve its neutrality in assessing adherence to the laws of war in the Iraq conflict, Human Rights Watch did not take a position on whether the war itself was justified or legal.

"Coalition forces generally tried to avoid killing Iraqis who weren't taking part in combat," said Kenneth Roth, executive director of Human Rights Watch. "But the deaths of hundreds of civilians still could have been prevented."[17]

Air attacks on leadership targets, like those launched in Iraq, should not be carried out until the intelligence and targeting failures have been corrected. Leadership strikes should not be carried out without an adequate collateral damage estimate (CDE).[18]

This style of criticism is perfectly functional. To establish your own neutrality, you start off by finding fault with your own side, deploring the death of a (greatly underestimated) number of civilian victims (there have been tens of thousands), which seem relatively few measured in terms of various other genocides and wars. Next, "neutrality" regarding the war goes so far as to agree to killing the leaders of the opposite side, just so long as the intelligence is correct and that the collateral damage is adequately evaluated (By whom? How? On what basis?).

Amnesty International and War

Amnesty also questioned whether the required precautions were being taken to protect civilians, and called for investigations into civilian deaths like those at the Karbala checkpoint, and the shooting of demonstrators in Falluja. But never once did Amnesty International ... mention the fundamental reason why none of the incidents really had to be investigated at all—namely that all of this death and destruction was legally, as well as morally, on the heads of the invaders, whatever precautions they claimed to take, because it was due to an illegal, aggressive war. Every death was a crime for which the leaders of the invading coalition were personally, criminally responsible.[19]

～

What the world needs today, alongside those organizations, would be an observatory to report on imperialism, a sort of "Imperialism Watch," whose job would be to denounce not only wars and war propaganda but all the economic pressures and various other maneuvers thanks to which injustice prospers and endures. Such an observatory could also try to counter the mass of disinformation and rewriting of history that characterize Western perceptions of the relations between ourselves and the rest of the world.

To a certain extent, that is the task undertaken by Al Jazeera and by what is sometimes called "Al Bolivar," that is, the new Latin American television station Telesur. These media can be seen as an extension of the appeal in favor of a new information world order launched by UNESCO and the countries of the South in the 1980s.[20] The Western reactions to Al Jazeera are amusing to observe. At first they tended to welcome the appearance in the Arab world of a "professional" network up to "Western" standards of objectivity, not subjected to state control and expressing itself freely without stereotypes. But then it became clear that this network was, nevertheless, Arab. That is, it did not necessarily present Israeli and Palestinian victims in the way our media do, it allowed all the belligerents to have their say—including bin Laden—and also had a tendency to present the Iraq resistance for what it is, that is, a national resistance rather than terrorism. Abruptly, the honeymoon between the West and Al Jazeera was over.

That interrupted honeymoon illustrates a broader phenomenon. Democracy in the Arab world, which Westerners claim to love so much, would be the worst catastrophe that could happen there, because what the peoples of the region want is a better price for their oil, a more economical management of that resource, and more active solidarity with the Palestinian cause. This is by no means what we want, and as for oil, it is by no means obvious that our extravagant economies and the institutions that depend on them could survive very long if that resource were truly controlled by the producing countries.

Vietnam's Independence

On September 2, 1945, after the defeat of the Japanese invader and before the French attempt to reconquer Indochina, President Ho Chi Minh proclaimed the following Declaration of Independence of the Democratic Republic of Vietnam:

"All men are created equal. They are endowed by their Creator with certain unalienable rights, among these are Life, Liberty, and the pursuit of Happiness."

This immortal statement was made in the Declaration of Independence of the United States of America in 1776. In a broader sense, this means: All the peoples on earth are equal from birth, all the peoples have a right to live, to be happy and free.

The Declaration of the Rights and the Citizen of the French Revolution of 1791 also proclaims: "All men are born and remain free and equal of rights."

These are undeniable truths.

Nevertheless, for more than eighty years, the French imperialists, abusing the standard of Liberty, Equality and Fraternity, have violated our Fatherland and oppressed our fellow-citizens. Their acts are the opposite of the ideals of humanity and justice.

In the field of politics, they deprived us of all liberties. They have enforced inhuman laws; they have set up three distinct political regimes in the North, the Center and the South of Vietnam in order to wreck our national unity and prevent our people from being united.

They have built more prisons than schools. They have mercilessly slain our patriots; they have drowned our uprisings in rivers of blood. They have fettered public opinion; they have practiced obscurantism against our people. To weaken our race they have forced us to use opium and alcohol.

In the economic field, they have fleeced us to the backbone, impoverished our people, and devastated our land.

They have robbed us of our rice fields, our mines, our forests, our raw materials. They have monopolized the issuing of bank-notes and the export trade. They have invented numerous unjustifiable taxes and reduced our people, especially our peasantry, to a state of extreme poverty. They have prevented our national bourgeoisie from prospering. They have exploited our workers in the most barbarian way.

For these reasons, we, members of the Provisional Government of the Democratic Republic of Vietnam, solemnly declare to the world that:

Vietnam has the right to be a free and independent country; and in fact is so already. The entire Vietnamese people are determined to mobilize all their physical and mental strength, to sacrifice their lives and property in order to safeguard their independence and liberty.

∽

And As for Hope?

All the colonized peoples have been able to turn the principles claimed by the colonizers against them. And the Iraqis could today make statements similar to those of the Vietnamese (even certain details like "setting up three political regimes in the North, the Center and the South"). The Israelis and their champions draw attention to human rights violations in

Arab countries in order to distract attention from international law or U.N. resolutions, which are not in their favor; but the occupation of Palestinian territories creates a cycle of violence and repression that is structurally incompatible with respect for human rights. The constant reference to human rights turns against them in the end.

We see a similar phenomenon concerning international criminal justice. This was conceived by the dominant powers essentially as a weapon against the leaders of weak but recalcitrant countries (Milosevic, for example) and as a means to legitimize intervention and even war.[21] But the intrinsically universal character of justice means that this weapon will eventually turn, at least on the level of discourse, against the powerful states and against men such as Olmert, Bush, and Blair.

Therefore, to function as an instrument of domination, the human rights ideology calls for rewriting history, selective indignation, and arbitrary priorities. The paradox is that the more ethics advances toward a genuine universality—and the human rights ideology constitutes an advance in relation to previous ideologies—the more hypocritical the dominant power becomes. The current dominant powers have a more universalist discourse than, say, Genghis Khan; as a result, they need to be more hypocritical.

But this implies also that denunciation of hypocrisy and demystification should play an increasingly important role, in particular, in critiques of the media and dominant intellectuals. The first sign of hope is that they are not as all-powerful as they tend to seem. In France, the media and the dominant intellectuals overwhelmingly supported a "yes" vote in the May 2005 referendum on the Treaty for a European Constitution, yet the "no" vote won a clear victory. In Venezuela, the press is almost entirely run by and for the opposition, but Chávez wins time and again. Even in the United States, despite insistence by media and both mainstream parties to "stay the course," a majority of the population seems to be fed up with the war in Iraq.

Recall that in 1991, after the collapse of the Soviet Union, America's world domination and the victory of the most unrestrained capitalism seemed final. Nevertheless, hope is in the process of changing sides. After the massive February 2003 antiwar demonstrations, the *New York Times* suggested that there were, after all, still two opposing superpowers: the United States and world public opinion.[22] The "weapon of criticism" is reemerging against the force of weapons, and there is no telling where that can lead. In Latin America, neoliberal illusions have been discredited and the neocolonial system is being challenged in one place after another. The stubborn resistance of the Iraqis is shaking the certainties of the part of the world that calls itself civilized.

Unfortunately, there is a sort of race between those two superpowers, the United States and world public opinion. The question is no longer whether or not the United States can impose its hegemony on the rest of the world. Since 1945, U.S. domination has weakened, not only economically but even diplomatically and militarily. Just compare the ease with which the United States overthrew Mossadegh or Arbenz in the 1950s with the trouble it took to overthrow Saddam Hussein (two wars and thirteen years of embargo), not to mention the current Iranian regime or Hugo Chávez. Europe's submission persists, but out of a kind of ambiguous inertia. When Jacques Chirac spoke of a multipolar world in 2003, the French president was the only Western political leader who still seemed able to think for himself. Far from expressing nostalgia for France's past glory, Chirac was simply recognizing the inevitable limits of power. By taking on the world, the United States is going beyond those limits. The future is uncertain, but it may well be that the war in Iraq, far from affirming U.S. supremacy, turns out to be the swan song of American imperial domination.

The main problem is how the Americans react to the inevitable loss of their hegemony—by a soft landing or by an explosion of violence. If it is the latter, the use of nuclear weapons cannot be excluded. After all, the most recent Pentagon strategies call for such usage, even—or especially—against adversaries who have none of their own.[23] Empires often have a way of creating the conditions that bring about their own inevitable and catastrophic fall. The very fear of such catastrophe is one of the things that keeps them going toward the end.

People who have been appealing to human rights for thirty years in order to flatter the American superpower risk finding themselves, perhaps against their will, the "objective allies" of monstrous undertakings.[24] In any case, the question of the "soft landing" is the major political problem of our time, as well as the principal challenge that needs to be met by progressive, peace, or global justice movements.

Let us look at history in the long term. At the beginning of the twentieth century, all of Africa and part of Asia were in the hands of European powers. The Russian, Chinese, and Ottoman empires were helpless in the face of Western interventions. Latin America was more tightly controlled than today. Of course, not everything has changed, but with the exception of Palestine, colonialism has at least been relegated to the ashcan of history, at the cost of millions of lives. This end of colonialism constitutes humanity's greatest social progress of the twentieth century. Those who want to revive the colonial system in Iraq, even with what Lord Curzon described, in the days of the British-controlled monarchy, an "Arab facade," are dreaming.[25] The twenty-first century will be that of the struggle against neocolonialism, just as the twentieth was the century of struggle against colonialism.

Insofar as the progress of the majority of humanity is linked to European defeats in the colonial conflicts, a narrowly Eurocentrist viewpoint leads us to see the evolution of the world in terms of decadence, which is no doubt one of the profound sources of the pessimism that characterizes the views of so many Western intellectuals. But another vision is possible. During the whole colonial period, we Europeans thought we could dominate the world by terror and force. Our absurd sense of superiority and our determination to impose our hegemony led us finally to slaughter each other, along with a good part of the rest of the world, during two world wars.

All those who prefer peace to power, and happiness to glory, should thank the colonized peoples for their civilizing mission. By liberating themselves, they made Europeans more modest, less racist, and more human. Let us hope that the process continues and that the Americans are obliged to follow the same course. When one's own cause is unjust, defeat can be liberating.

Notes

Preface

1. The Alliance of the victorious powers, Russia, Prussia, Austria and Great Britain, following the fall of Napoleon, which proclaimed a "right of intervention" allowing it to suppress popular national aspirations and insurrections in Europe.

2. Serge Halimi provides a good analysis of that evolution in his book, *Le grand bond en arrière. Comment l'ordre libéral s'est imposé au monde*, Paris, Fayard, 2004.

3. For a criticism of certain forms of relativism, see: Alan Sokal, Jean Bricmont, *Fashionable Nonsense: Postmodern Intellectuals' Abuse of Science*, New York, Picador, 1997; and Régis Debray, Jean Bricmont, *À l'ombre des Lumières*, Paris, Odile Jacob, 2003.

4. For a good analysis of the neoconservative philosophy, see Shadia B. Drury, *Leo Strauss and the American Right*, New York, St. Martin's Press, 1999.

5. My text, "Why we still need to be anti-imperialists," is available in the electronic publication of CEIMSA, *La Publication des Actes du Colloque des 11–12 janvier 2002*, Chapter 25, to be found under the heading "Colloques" on the site: <http://dimension.ucsd.edu/CEIMSA-IN-EXILE/>. Also available on: http://www. zmag. org/content/TerrorWar/bricmontimperial.cfm.

Introduction

1. Bertrand Russell, *The Practice and Theory of Bolshevism* (London: Allen and Unwin, 1920). During the First World War, the Entente was made up of England, France, and (until the October Revolution) Russia, opposed to the Central German and Austro-Hungarian empires.

2. I have also taken part in the Brussels Tribunal (http://www.brusselstribunal.org), a section of the World Tribunal on Iraq (http://www.worldtribunal.org), which is set up to judge the crimes committed by the United States and their allies in Iraq.

3. U.S. Department of Defense, *National Defense Strategy of the United States of America,* March 2005, available on http://www.stormingmedia.us/41/4121/A412134.html, or http://www.globalsecurity.org/military/library/policy/dod/nds-usa_mar2005.htm.

4. In particular, see "new philosophers" Pascal Bruckner, *The Tears of the White Man: Compassion as Contempt* (New York: Macmillan, 1986); and Bernard-Henri Lévy, *La barbarie à visage humain* (Paris: Grasset, 1977). It is worth noting that the second book is not, as is sometimes assumed, a simple critique of Stalinism but rather an all-out attack against the very idea of progress.

5. Russell, *Practice and Theory of Bolshevism,* 85.

6. John A. Hobson, a reformist British economist, wrote one of the first critical works on imperialism: *Imperialism, A Study* (New York: James Pott and Co., 1902). This work had a strong influence on Lenin.

7. Yaroslav Trofimov, *Wall Street Journal,* September 18, 2001. If the *Wall Street Journal*'s reporters are surprised by the reactions to September 11 in the Arab world, it may well be because they share with Marxists the idea that self-enrichment is the "natural aim of man's political action."

1.Power and Ideology

1. Bertrand Russell, *Freedom and Organization, 1814–1914* (London: Routledge, 2001), 45–473.

2. Arthur Schlessinger, *New York Times*, February 6, 1966.

3. Shannon, *New York Times*, September 28, 1974, cited by Noam Chomsky in *Human Rights and American Foreign Policy* (Nottingham, Eng.: Spokesman Books, 1978), 2–3. Available at http://book-case.kroupnov.ru/pages/library/HumanRights/.

4. This letter, justifying the U.S. invasion of Afghanistan, was signed by sixty intellectuals, including Francis Fukuyama, Samuel Huntington, Daniel Patrick Moynihan, and Michael Walzer. So far, the Muslim "brothers and sisters" do not seem to have been impressed by this display of altruism. The full text is available at http://www.americanvalues.org/html/wwff.html.

5. "Secular priesthood" is an expression coined by Isaiah Berlin ("The Bent Twig," *Foreign Affairs*, October 1977) who was referring to the Communist intelligentsia in the socialist countries.

2. The Third World and the West

1. See http://members.aol.com/Bblum6/American_holocaust.htm.

2. It is true that there are other Third World leaders, less admirable than those mentioned here, who are also opposed by the West, a matter touched upon in point 3 that follows.

3. Jean Drèze and Amartya Sen, *Hunger and Public Action* (Oxford, Eng.: Clarendon Press, 1989), 214–15.

4 Under-five mortality measures the number of children per thousand who die in their first five years of life. For Cuba and Latin America, the rate is respectively 9 and 34 (Human Development Report 2004, pp.169 and 171). The number of children who could be saved is calculated on the basis of the difference between the rate of mortality multiplied by the birth rate (22 per thousand) and the number of inhabitants (518.9 million). See also : The state of the world's children 2007. The Double Dividend of Gender Equality. http://www.unicef.org/sowc07/docs/sowc07. pdf, p. 102 & 105.

5   ILO, The end of child labour: Within reach. Genève 2006, http://www.ilo.org/public/ english/standards/relm/ilc/ilc95/pdf/rep-i- b.pdf , p. 8.

6   "UNICEF reports that there are 100 million street children in the world, of which half are found in Latin America," quoted in: *Street Children in Central America: An Overview.* Miki Takahashi and Caroline Cederlof, Human Development Department, World bank, http://lnweb18.worldbank.org/external/lac/lac.nsf/0/19e661ab-7bbb25de852568cf006ad8a8?OpenDocument

7. A conference held in Bandung (Indonesia) in 1955 brought together some thirty newly independent Asian and African countries. Among those participating were Nehru for India, Nasser for Egypt, and Zhou Enlai for China. It marked the birth of the Third World as a political entity. It called for decolonization, peaceful cooperation, nonalignment, and respect for national sovereignty.

8. Michael Ignatieff, "The Burden," *The New York Times Magazine,* January 5, 2003.

9. Noam Chomsky, "Telling the Truth about Imperialism," *International Socialist Review,* November–December 2003, available at http://www.chomsky.info/interviews/ 200311—.htm.

10. Thomas L. Friedman, *The New York Times Magazine,* March 28, 1999.

11. See Arno J. Mayer, *The Furies: Violence and Terror in the French and Russian Revolutions* (Princeton, N.J.: Princeton University Press, 2000). Mayer cites the "approximate figures" in Robert Conquest, *The Harvest of Sorrow: Soviet Collectivisation and the Terror Famine* (New York: Oxford University Press, 1986), 53–54: two million dead in the First World War; one million in the first phase of the

civil war; two million in the peasant wars; three million dead of disease and five million of famine. Russia was the only principal belligerent to lose more civilians than soldiers in World War I. In World War II, Soviet deaths are estimated at over twenty million.

12. The Versailles Treaty, signed in June 1919, formally ended World War I. It imposed on Germany full responsibility for the war, the loss of territory and colonies, partial demilitarization, and heavy reparations payments. The Austro-Hungarian and Ottoman Empires were dismantled.

13. Russell, *Practice and Theory of Bolshevism*, 55.

14. *International Herald Tribune*, October 29, 1992, cited by William Blum, *Killing Hope: U.S. Military and CIA Interventions since World War II* (Monroe, Me.: Common Courage Press, 1995).

15. Facts taken from United Nations Development Program, "Human Development Report" (2005).

16. In 1916, the secret Sykes-Picot Accord between Great Britain and France defined the way those two countries would divide up the Middle East after the fall of the Ottoman Empire. This accord betrayed the promises made to Arab leaders (to get them to fight the Ottoman Turks) and was revealed by the Bolsheviks after the Russian Revolution. In 1956, in an attempt to stop Egyptian president Nasser's nationalization of the Suez Canal, France, Britain, and Israel attacked Egypt, but the United States and the Soviet Union forced them to back down.

17. A few examples are the 1871 Paris Commune, which originated as a defensive movement against Prussian occupation; the Chinese Communist Revolution, a defensive movement against Japanese invasion; and the violence of the Khmer Rouge, a reaction to years of U.S. clandestine bombing of the Cambodian countryside.

18. See Blum, *Killing Hope,* chap. 9, for the overthrow of Mossadegh; and chap. 12 for the failed attempt to overthrow the Syrian regime.

19. Cited by Noam Chomsky, *"Human Rights" and American Foreign Policy* (Nottingham, Eng.: Spokesman Books, 1978), 18.

20. Kautsky, a theoretician of German social democracy, is best known by the epithet "renegade," attributed to him by Lenin. But his work *Terrorism and Communism* (to which Trotsky replied with a work of his own with the same title), although it suffers from the optimistic illusions current in the Second International, nevertheless contains an interesting critique of Bolshevik ideas, in particular dictatorship.

21. The United States considered Cambodia's popular ruling prince too neutralist in regard to the war in Vietnam. Thus in 1970, Prince Sihanouk was overthrown by General Lon Nol with the support of the United States. Lon Nol's brutal and unpopular rule contributed to the Khmer Rouge victory in 1975.

22. Diana Johnstone, *Fools' Crusade: Yugoslavia, NATO and Western Delusions* (New York: Monthly Review Press/London: Pluto Press, 2002), 43–44.

23. Michael Mandel, *How America Gets Away With Murder* (London: Pluto Press, 2004), 67.

24. See, for example, *Washington Post*, March 11, 1999, available at http://www.washingtonpost.com:wpsrv/inatl/daukt/larcg99/ckubtib11.htm.

25. The web site "Economy in Crisis" (http://www.economyincrisis.org/) gives numerous figures illustrating the growing dependence of the United States on Asia (debt, sales of companies, loss of competition, etc.).

26. Thomas L. Friedman, "Fly Me to the Moon," *New York Times*, December 5, 2004.

27. Jamie Wilson, "U.S. Military Sends Scientists to Film School," *The Guardian*, August 5, 2005.

28. It is significant that the Shanghai Cooperation Organization, made up of China, Russia, and four former Soviet Republics, in the summer of 2005 called on the United States to set a timetable for withdrawal of their troops from Central Asia. See, for example, Siddarth Varadarajan, "China, Russia Get Central Asians to say 'Yankees Out!'," *The Hindu*, July 7, 2005.

29. "Missile defense isn't really meant to protect America. It's a tool for global dominance." It is "not about defense. It's about offense. And that's exactly why we need it." It will provide the U.S. with "absolute freedom in using or threatening to use force in international relations." It will "cement U.S. hegemony and make Americans 'masters of the world.'" Lawrence F. Kaplan, "Offensive Line," *The New Republic* 224 (March 12, 2001), quoted in Noam Chomsky, *Hegemony or Survival: America's Quest for Global Dominance* (New York: Metropolitan Books, 2003).

30. See http://www.casi.org.uk/halliday/quotes.html.

31. Report by Marc Bossuyt, "The Adverse Consequences of Economic Sanctions on the Enjoyment of Human Rights," to the United Nations Human Rights Commission, June 21, 2000. Available at: http://www.globalpolicy.org/security/sanction/unreports/bossuyt.htm.

32. John A. Hobson, *Imperialism, A Study* (New York: James Pott and Co., 1902).

33. This section is based on Piero Gleijeses, *Shattered Hope. The Guatemalan Revolution and the United States, 1944–1954* (Princeton, N.J.: Princeton University Press, 1991); and Edward S. Herman, "From Guatemala to Iraq. How the Pitbull Manages His Poodles," *Z Magazine*, January 2003, available at http://zmagsite.zmag.org/jan2003/herman0103.shtm.

3. Questions to Human Rights Defenders

1. Thomas Cushman ed., *A Matter of Principle: Humanitarian Arguments for War in Iraq* (Berkeley: University of California Press, 2005). Contributors include Tony Blair, Christopher Hitchens, Adam Michnik (who became known as an intellectual supporter of Polish Solidarnosc) and José Ramos Horta, 1996 Nobel Peace Prize winner for his commitment to independence for East Timor.

2. *The Euston Manifesto*, March 29, 2006. At http://www.eustonmanifesto.org/.

3. Letter to President Clinton, January 28, 1998, and signed by: Elliott Abrams, Richard L. Armitage, William J. Bennett, Jeffrey Bergner, John Bolton, Paula Dobriansky, Francis Fukuyama, Robert Kagan, Zalmay Khalilzad, William Kristol, Richard Perle, Peter W. Rodman, Donald Rumsfeld, William Schneider, Jr., Vin Weber, Paul Wolfowitz, R. James Woolsey, Robert B. Zoellick, many of whom have at some time held high positions in the Bush administration. Available at http://www.newamericancentury.org.

4. "Human rights is the soul of our foreign policy. And I say this with assurance, because human rights is the soul of our sense of nationhood. . . . Uniquely, ours is a nation founded on an idea of human rights." From "The U.S. Commitment: Human Rights and Foreign Policy," remarks by President Jimmy Carter at a White House meeting for the thirtieth anniversary of the signing of the Universal Declaration of Human Rights, December 1978; available at http://usinfo.state.gov/products/pubs/hrintro/carter.htm. President of the United States from 1977 to 1980, an apparently sincere Christian with little foreign affairs experience before his election, Carter was certainly one of the most appealing U.S. presidents, especially for what he has done since leaving office. He is also one of the least popular. In France, the media and political class much preferred the supposedly worldly realpolitik of a Kissinger. Regardless of his good intentions, Carter ended up as the "useful idiot" of the Trilateral Commission, David Rockefeller and Zbigniew Brzezinski, helping Vietnam be forgotten thanks to his moralizing, before the return to business as usual under Reagan, president from 1981 to 1988.

5. Interview with Zbigniew Brzezinski, *Le Nouvel Observateur* (Paris), January 15–21, 1998, 76. (Trans. from the French by author.)

6. Bernard Kouchner, *Les Guerriers de la Paix* (Paris : Grasset, 2004), 373–74.

7. On the application of the "Salvador option" to Iraq, that is, the utilization of death squads to eliminate the civilian resistance, see Mussab Al-Khairall, "U.N. Raises Alarm on Death Squads and Torture in Iraq," Reuters, September 8, 2005; for a detailed analysis, see Max Fuller, "For Iraq, 'The Salvador Option' Becomes Reality," available at http:/globalresearch.ca/articles/FUL506A.html.

8. George Will, "A War President's Job," *The Washington Post*, April 7, 2004.

9. See Edward S. Herman and Noam Chomsky, *Manufacturing Consent* (New York: Pantheon, 2002), for a detailed analysis of media distortion in a free society.

10. Les Roberts et al., "Mortality Before and After the 2003 Invasion of Iraq: Cluster Sample Survey," *The Lancet* 364 (November 20, 2004). A new study, published when the English translation of this book was done, puts the death toll above 600,000, see http://web.mit.edu/CIS/pdf/Human_Cost_of_War.pdf.

11. For media treatment of the study, see Media Lens at http://www.medialens.org/alerts/archive_2005.php.

12. See the site of families who have become active for peace after having lost a member in the war: http://www.gsfp.org/.

13. Available at http://www.washingtonpost.com/wp-dyn/content/article/2005/09/03/AR2005090300165.html.

14. Stead, *Die Neue Zeit*, 1898, 16th year, no. 1, 304, cited by Lenin in *Imperialism: The Highest Stage of Capitalism*.

15. Amy Wilentz, *The New Republic*, March 9, 1992. Also see Noam Chomsky, *Rogue States; The Rule of Force in World Affairs* (Boston: South End Press, 2000), chap. 10.

16. Available at http://news.bbc.co.uk/2/hi/middle_east/4151742.stm.

17. Alan M. Dershowitz, "New Response to Palestinian Terrorism," *Jerusalem Post*, March 11, 2002.

18. See Richard B. DuBoff, *Accumulation and Power: An Economic History of the United States* (New York and London: M.E.Sharpe/Armonk, 1989).

19. For an enumeration of U.S. military budget items, see Winslow T. Wheeler, "Just How Big Is the Defense Budget? A Tutorial on How to Find the Real Numbers," *Counterpunch*, January 19, 2006: "If you count all these costs, the total is $669.8 billion. This amount easily outdoes the rest of the world. In fact, if you count just the costs of the National Defense budget function, the approximate $538 billion we spend is $29 billion more than the $509 billion the entire rest of the world spends." Available at http://www.counterpunch.org/wheeler01192006.html.

20. Michael Neumann, "Michael Ignatieff, Apostle of He-manitarianism," *Counterpunch*, December 8, 2003; available at http://www.counterpunch.org/neumann12082003.html.

21. For the full story of the dismantling of Yugoslavia, see Johnstone, *Fools' Crusade: Yugoslavia, NATO and Western Delusions* (London: Pluto, 2002).

22. For an excellent analysis of the indirect effects of classic nineteenth-century colonialism, far worse than the direct effects, see Mike Davis, *Late Victorian Holocausts: El Nino, Famines and the Making of the Third World* (London/New York: Verso, 2001).

23. Excerpts from a speech given by former Malaysian prime minister Mohamed Mahathir at the Suhakam Human Rights Conference, September 9, 2005. During the speech, Western diplomats walked out. Available at http://informationclearinghouse.info/article 10305.htm.

24. For example, Article 22 of the Declaration states: "Everyone, as a member of society, has a right to social security and is entitled to realization, through national effort and international cooperation and in accordance with the organization and resources of each state, of the economic, social and cultural rights indispensable for his dignity and the free development of his personality."

25. Jeane J. Kirkpatrick, "Establishing a Viable Human Rights Policy," article presented to human rights conference, Kenyon College, April 4, 1981. The article is an attack on the "human rights policy" of the Carter administration, from a Reaganite point of view. "Such declarations of human 'rights' take on the character of 'a letter to Santa Claus'—as Orwin and Prangle noted. They can multiply indefinitely because 'no clear standard informs them, and no great reflection produced them.' For every goal human beings have worked toward, there is in our time a 'right.' Neither nature, experience, nor probability informs these lists of 'entitlements,' which are subject to no constraints except those of the mind and appetite of their authors. The fact that such entitlements may be without possibility of realization does not mean they are without consequences."

26. For details, see William Blum, *Rogue State: A Guide to the World's Only Superpower* (Monroe, Me.: Common Courage Press, 2005), 168–78.

27. "Erst kommt das fressen, dann kommt die Moral." Brecht, *Drei Groschen Oper.*

28. For example, the International Federation of Human Rights Leagues (FIDH) and the French League of the Rights of Man and of the Citizen (LDH) issued a statement stressing that "civil, political, economic, social and cultural rights are indivisible, democracy, development and human rights are interdependent. The experience of the practices ascribed to the Tunisian regime demonstrate how much economic development does not at all lead to improvement with respect to civil and political rights but on the contrary serves as a pretext to legitimatize their violation." However, in the case of the West, it is indeed "economic development" that preceded "improvement with respect to civil and political rights."

29. It is said that in his youth Chirac peddled the Communist newspaper *L'Humanité* on street corners. Perhaps of the two, he has changed the least.

30. Nevertheless, as an example of tit for tat, see the Chinese report of violations of human rights in the United States, as well as in the course of U.S. wars: http://english.people.com.cn/ 200503/03/eng20050303_175406.html.

4. Weak and Strong Arguments against War

1. In September 1938, Hitler, Mussolini, Chamberlain (for Great Britain), and Daladier (for France) signed the Munich Agreement that allowed Germany to annex part of Czechoslovakia, the Sudeten region, populated mainly by Germans who considered themselves persecuted by the Czechs and welcomed the German troops. Weakened by this annexation, Czechoslovakia as a whole was annexed by Germany in March 1939.

2. See Mandel, *How America Gets Away with Murder: Illegal Wars, Collateral Damage and Crimes against Humanity* (London: Pluto Press, 2004) for a detailed argument on that issue.

3. In 1940, the year before Pearl Harbor, U.S. Air Force General Chenneault recommended using flying fortresses "to burn out the industrial heart of the Empire" by dropping incendiary bombs "on the teeming bamboo ant heaps" of Japan, a proposal that "simply delighted" Roosevelt. Saddam Hussein never expressed such warlike intentions against the United States. See Michael Sherry, *The Rise of American Airpower* (New Haven: Yale University Press, 1987), chap. 4; and Noam Chomsky, "The Manipulation of Fear," *Tehelka*, July 16, 2005, available at http://www.chomsky.info/articles/20050716.htm.

4. See Chalmers Johnson, *Blowback: The Costs and Consequences of American Empire* (New York: Metropolitan Books, 2000), for a warning, written by a former CIA consultant before September 11, about the risks posed to the United States by its empire.

5. *Washington Post*, September 14, 1969, cited by William Blum, *Killing Hope: U.S. Military and CIA Interventions since World War II* (Monroe, Me.: Common Courage Press, 1995).

6. Excerpt from final document of the Thirteenth Conference of Heads of State and of Governments of the Movement of Non-aligned Countries, Kuala Lumpur, February 24–25, 2003, Article 354. Available at http://www.bernama.com/events/newnam2003/indexspeech.shtml?declare.

7. Edward S. Herman, "Michael Ignatieff's Pseudo-Hegelian Apologetics for Imperialism," *Z Magazine,* October 2005. See also William Blum, *Rogue State: A Guide to the World's Only Superpower* (Monroe, Me.: Common Courage Press, 2005), for numerous examples; and Stephen Zunes, *Tinderbox: U.S. Foreign Policy and the Roots of Terrorism* (Monroe, Me.: Common Courage Press, 2002), for an account of how José Bustani, who directed the Organization for Prohibition of Chemical Weapons, was fired under United States influence the moment he wanted to have both American and Iraqi sites inspected, which might have had the disadvantage of allowing a peaceful resolution of the conflict. See also Richard Du Boff,

"Mirror Mirror on the Wall, Who's the Biggest Rogue of All?" for a more complete and detailed list of the treaties and accords rejected by the United States. See http://www.zmag.org/content/ForeignPolicy/boffroguebig.cfm.

8. Daniel P. Moynihan and S. Weaver, *A Dangerous Place* (London: Secker and Warburg, 1979).

9. Available at http://www.americanvalues.org/html/wwff.html. A response, entitled "Letter from American citizens to their friends in Europe," signed by 140 intellectuals, stressed: "The central fallacy of the pro-war celebrants is the equation between 'American values' as understood at home and the exercise of United States economic and especially military power abroad." This letter was published in a number of European newspapers, including *Le Monde*, *Frankfurter Rundschau*, and *Süddeutsche Zeitung*. It was reproduced in *L'Autre Amérique: Les Américains contre l'état de guerre* (Paris: Textuel, 2002).

10. See Blum, *Rogue State*, 185–97, for many similar examples.

11. This is a total fantasy—the Sandinistas never made such a claim.

12. Blum, *Rogue State*, 47.

13. Alexandre Adler, "Les tentations de Chávez," *Le Figaro* (Paris), May 11, 2005.

5. Illusions and Mystifications

1. See Robert Fisk, "The Wartime Deceptions: Saddam Is Hitler and It's Not About Oil," *Independent* (London), January 27, 2003.

2. Andrew Sullivan, former editor of *The New Republic*, quoted in Anatol Lieven, *America Right or Wrong: An Anatomy of American Nationalism* (Oxford: Oxford University Press, 2004).

3. See, for example, Thomas Cushman, ed., *A Matter of Principle: Humanitarian Arguments for War in Iraq* (Berkeley: University of California Press, 2005).

4. Full text is available at http://www.mae.es/index2.jsp?URL=Buscar.jsp.

5. From *Proceso,* journal of the Jesuit University of El Salvador, cited by Noam Chomsky, *Deterring Democracy* (New York: Vintage,1992), 354–55.

6. Tony Judt, "Bush's Useful Idiots," *London Review of Books*, September 21, 2006.

6. The Guilt Weapon

1. Vernon Loeb, "Afghan Combat a Lab for Honing Military Technology," *Washington Post,* March 28, 2002; available at www.dawn.com/2002/03/28/int14.htm.

2. This and other memos dealing with the same subject and going back to March 2002 (that is, well before all the debates on the need to disarm Iraq) are available at http://www.downingstreetmemo.com/memos.html.

3. Jaurès was assassinated on July 31, 1914, on the eve of the war. Liebknecht and Luxemburg, German social democrats opposed to the war, were murdered in 1919.

   When Bertrand Russell sought to convince the United States to help work out a compromise in Europe rather than enter the war, his colleague Alfred North Whitehead, with whom he had written his major work *Principia Matematica*, sent him reports on victims of German atrocities with the comment that those who wanted America to remain neutral were responsible for their fate, adding, "What are *you* going to do to help these people?" Ray Monk, *Bertrand Russell, the Spirit of Solitude* (London: Random House/Vintage, 1997), 487.

   Edmund Morel was an Anglo-French journalist and political figure who denounced the exactions of Leopold II in the Belgian Congo and opposed the First World War. He was imprisoned in Britain for having mailed pacifist literature to the novelist Romain Rolland in Switzerland, a neutral country, in violation of certain wartime measures.

   Eugene Debs, labor leader and cofounder of the American Socialist Party, was sentenced to ten years in prison in 1918 for antimilitarism.

4. This distinction is deliberately blurred when genuine civil conflict within a country, notably the wars of Yugoslav disintegration, is presented as "outside aggression," in order to justify real outside intervention. See Diana Johnstone, *Fools' Crusade: Yugoslavia, NATO and Western Delusions* (New York: Monthly Review Press/London: Pluto Press, 2002),169: "Rapid recognition of Croatia and Slovenia was designed *not*—as officially claimed by the German government—to *prevent* military conflict, but to *internationalize* it, in order to justify outside military intervention, *with German participation*." The same device was used when Yugoslavia's suppression of Albanian secession in Kosovo was presented as a Serbian "invasion" of its own territory.

5. See Noam Chomsky, *Language and Politics*, ed. C. P. Otero (Montreal: Black Rose Books, 1988), 204–8, for a more thorough discussion.

6. More than simply refusing to help "heal the wounds of war" (as the Vietnamese tactfully put it), in 1977 the United States tried to prevent India from sending a hundred buffalo to Vietnam (whose livestock had been decimated by U.S. bombing), and also tried to prohibit American Mennonites from sending pencils to Cambodia and shovels to Laos. See *The Chomsky Reader*, ed. James Peck (New York: Pantheon Books, 1987), 326.

7. See Naomi Klein, "Baghdad Year Zero," *Harper's*, September 2004 (available at http://harpers.org/BaghdadYearZero.html), for a sarcastic description of American

companies' behavior, which ended in a general rout when the Iraqi resistance and the chaos in the country made pillage more difficult.

8. Salman Rushdie, "How to Fight and Lose the Moral High Ground," *Guardian*, March 23, 2002.

9. In 1935, when the French prime minister Pierre Laval asked Stalin to restore good relations with the Vatican, Stalin is said to have replied: "The Pope, how many divisions?"

10. Thomas L. Friedman, "Bush's Radically Liberal War in Iraq Is No Vietnam," *New York Times*, October 31, 2003.

7. Prospects, Dangers and Hopes

1. These lies were authoritatively exposed by a retired German General who had served with the Organization for Security and Cooperation in Europe (OSCE) during the Yugoslav crisis. Heinz Loquai, *Der Kosovo-Konflikt—Wege in einen vermeidbaren Krieg* [The Kosovo Conflict: Paths to an Avoidable War] (Baden-Baden: Nomos Verlagsgesellschaft, 2000). For background of the Kosovo war, see Diana Johnstone, *Fool's Crusade: Yugoslavia, NATO and Western Delusions* (London: Pluto, 2002).

2. Peter Beaumont, "PM Admits Graves Claim 'Untrue'," *Observer*, July 18, 2004. Note that they forget to mention the Vietnam War in which deaths were in the millions, not the hundreds of thousands.

3. See http://uslaboragainstwar.org/article.php ?id=8626.

4. For example, in mid-September 2005, the Interior Ministry of Italy refused to grant visas to a number of representatives of movements and associations opposed to the Iraqi government and to the occupation who had hoped to come to Italy to attend a conference in support of the Iraqi resistance. *Il Manifesto*, September 14, 2005.

5. "The front page story in the *New York Times* reported "Patients and hospital employees were rushed out of rooms by armed soldiers and ordered to sit or lie on the floor while troops tied their hands behind their backs." An accompanying photograph depicted the scene. That was presented as a meritorious achievement. "The offensive also shut down what officers said was a propaganda weapon for the militants: Falluja General Hospital, with its stream of reports of civilian casualties." Plainly such a propaganda weapon is a legitimate target, particularly when "inflated civilian casualty figures"—inflated because our leader so declares—were "inflaming opinion throughout the country, driving up the political costs of the conflict." The word "conflict" is a common euphemism for U.S. aggression, as when we read on

the same pages that the U.S. must now rebuild "what the conflict just destroyed": just "the conflict," with no agent, like a hurricane." Noam Chomsky, *Failed States. The Abuse of Power and the Assault on Democracy* (New York: Metropolitan Books, 2006), 47–48.

6. David Baran, "Iraq: the Fear of Chaos," *Le Monde Diplomatique*, December 2003.

7. See http://www.brusselstribunal.org/.

8. John McNaughton, CIA analyst, text from the Pentagon Papers quoted in Noam Chomsky, *For Reasons of State* (New York: New Press, 2003), 67.

9. Michael Mandel, *How America Gets Away With Murder: Illegal Wars, Collateral Damage and Crimes against Humanity* (London: Pluto Press, 2004).

10. "Open Letter to Amnesty International on the Iraqi Constitution," published by the Brussels Tribunal (www.brusselstribunal.org).

11. Noam Chomsky, "On the War in Iraq," interview with David McNeill, *ZNet*, January 31, 2005.

12. Johann Hari, "After Three Years, After 150,000 Dead, Why I Was Wrong about Iraq: A Melancholic Mea Culpa," *Independent* (London), March 18, 2006. On his own web site, Hari writes modestly that "Johann has been attacked in print by the Daily Telegraph, John Pilger, Peter Oborne, *Private Eye*, the *Socialist Worker*, Cristina Odone, the *Spectator*, Andrew Neil, Mark Steyn, the British National Party, Medialens, al Muhajaroun and Richard Littlejohn. 'Prince' Turki al-Faisal, the Saudi ambassador to Britain, has accused Johann of 'waging a private jihad against the House of Saud.' (He's right). Johann has been called 'a Stalinist' and 'beneath contempt' by Noam Chomsky, 'Horrible Hari' by Niall Ferguson, 'an uppity little queer' by Bruce Anderson, 'a drug addict' by George Galloway, 'fat' by the Dalai Lama and 'a cunt' by Busted." Now, he is called deluded, but by himself.

13. Rick Klein, "Democrats Embrace Tough Military Stance," *Boston Globe*, August 14, 2005. Available at http://www.boston.com/news/nation/washington/articles/2005/08/14/democrats_embrace_tough_military_stance/?page=1.

14. Ari Berman, "The Strategic Class," *The Nation*, August 29, 2005.

15. An example of this attitude is expressed by Paul Craig Roberts, a former assistant secretary of the Treasury in the Reagan administration, a former associate editor of the *Wall Street Journal* editorial page, and a former contributing editor for *National Review*. See http://www.lewrockwell.com/roberts/roberts-arch.html.

16. Posted by Billmon on http://billmon.org/archives/002767.html.

17. Human Rights Watch press release, New York, December 12, 2003. One wonders how Roth knows the intentions of the coalition forces. The same type of problems

occurred during the 2006 Lebanon war; see Jonathan Cook, "Human Rights Watch: Still Missing the Point," available at http://www.counterpunch.org/cook09252006.html.

18. Summary and recommendations of Human Rights Watch, "Off Target: The Conduct of the War and Civilian Casualties in Iraq," available at http://hrw.org/reports/2003/usa1203/.

19. Michael Mandel, *How America Gets Away with Murder*, 8, quoted in Paul de Rooij, "Amnesty International: A False Beacon?," *Counterpunch*, October 13, 2004, http://www.counterpunch.org/rooij10132004.html.

20. See William Preston Jr., Edward S. Herman, Herbert I. Schiller, *Hope and Folly: The United States and UNESCO 1945–1985* (Minneapolis: University of Minnesota Press, 1989).

21. On the nature of international justice and the ideology of intervention that underlies it, see David Chandler, *From Kosovo to Kabul: Human Rights and International Intervention* (London: Pluto Press, 2002); Johnstone, *Fools' Crusade;* and Mandel, *How America Gets Away with Murder.*

22. Patrick Tyler, *New York Times*, February 17, 2003.

23. See Associated Press, "U.S. Nuke Arms Plan Envisions Pre-Emption," September 11, 2005.

24. For a similar judgment, see Tony Judt, "Bush's Useful Idiots," *London Review of Books,* September 21, 2006.

25. "[We need] an Arab facade ruled and administered under British guidance and controlled by a native Mohammedan and, as far as possible, by an Arab staff.... There should be no actual incorporation of the conquered territory in the dominions of the conqueror, but the absorption may be veiled by such constitutional fictions as a protectorate, a sphere of influence, a buffer state and so on." Memorandum of Lord Curzon, "German and Turkish Territories Captured in the War," December 12, 1917, CAB 24/4. Cited by William Stivers, *Supremacy and Oil: Iraq, Turkey, and the Anglo-American World Order, 1918–1930* (Ithaca, N.Y.: Cornell University Press, 1982).

Bibliography

Ali, Tariq, *The Clash of Fundamentalisms. Crusades, Jihads and Modernity*, London, Verso, 2002.

Ali, Tariq, *Bush in Babylon. The Recolonizattion of Iraq*, London, Verso, 2003.

Arnove, Anthony, *Iraq. The Logic of Withdrawal*, The New Press, New York, 2006.

Blum, William, *Rogue State. A Guide to the World's Only Superpower*, Monroe (Maine), Common Courage Press, 2005 (new edition).

Blum, William, *Killing Hope: U.S. Military and CIA Interventions since World War II*, Monroe (Maine), Common Courage Press, 2005 (updated edition).

Chandler, David, *From Kosovo to Kabul. Human Rights and International Intervention*, London, Pluto Press, 2002.

Chandler, David, (ed.), *Rethinking Human Rights: Critical Approaches to International Politics*, Houndmills (UK), Palgrave Macmillan, 2002.

Chomsky, Noam, *American Power and the New Mandarins*, New York, The New Press, 2002 (first edition : New York, Pantheon Books (Random House), 1969).

Chomsky, Noam, *For Reasons of State*, New York, The New Press, 2003 (first edition, New York, Pantheon Books (Random House), 1972).

Chomsky, Noam, Edward S. Herman, *The Washington Connection and Third World Fascism*, Boston, South End Press, 1980.

Chomsky, Noam, Edward S. Herman, *After the Cataclysm, Postwar Indochina and the Reconstruction of Imperial Ideology*, Boston, South End Press, 1979.

Chomsky, Noam, *'Human Rights' and American Foreign Policy*, Nottingham, Spokesman Books, 1978.

Chomsky, Noam, *Language and Politics*, ed. Carlos P. Otero, Montréal, Black Rose Books, 1988.

Chomsky, Noam, *Deterring Democracy*, New York, Vintage, 1992.

Chomsky, Noam, *Rogue States. The Rule of Force in World Affairs*, Boston, South End Press, 2000.

Chomsky, Noam, *Hegemony or Survival. America's Quest for Global Dominance*, New York, Metropolitan Books, 2003.

Cockburn, Alexander, *The Golden Age Is in Us*, London, Verso, 1995.

Cushman, Thomas (ed.), *A Matter of Principle. Humanitarian Arguments for War in Iraq*, Berkeley, University of California Press, 2005.

Davis, Mike, *Late Victorian Holocausts: El Nino Famines and the Making of the Third World*, London, Verso, 2002.

Delorca, Frédéric (ed.), *Atlas alternatif,* Paris, Le Temps des Cerises, 2005.

Drèze, Jean, Amartya Sen, *Hunger and Public Action*, Oxford, Clarendon Press, 1989.

DuBoff, Richard B., *Accumulation and Power: An Economic History of the United States*, New York, M.E. Sharpe, 1989.

Evans, Tony (ed.), *Human Rights Fifty Years On. A Reappraisal*, New York, St. Martin's Press, 1998.

Finkelstein, Norman, *Image and Reality of the Israel-Palestine Conflict*, London, Verso, 1995.

George, Alexander (ed.), *Western State Terrorism*, Cambridge, Polity Press, 1991.

Gleijeses, Piero, *Shattered Hope. The Guatemalan Revolution and the United States, 1944-1954*, Princeton, Princeton University Press, 1991.

Halimi, Serge, *Le grand bond en arrière. Comment l'ordre libéral s'est imposé au monde*, Paris, Fayard, 2004.

Herman, Edward S., *The Real Terror Network. Terrorism in Fact and Propaganda*, Boston, South End Press, 1982.

Herman, Edward S., Noam Chomsky, *Manufacturing Consent: The Political Economy of the Mass Media*, New York, Pantheon Books, 2002 (first edition, 1988).

Hobson, John A., *Imperialism, A Study*, New York, James Pott and Co., 1902, available on http://www.econlib.org/library/YPDBooks/Hobson/hbsnImp.html.

Hochschild, Adam, *King Leopold's Ghost: A Story of Greed, Terror, and Heroism in Colonial Africa*, New York, Mariner Books, 1999.

Johnson, Chalmers, *Blowback: The Costs and Consequences of American Empire*, New York, Metropolitan Books, 2000.

Johnstone, Diana, *Fool's Crusade. Yugoslavia, NATO and Western Delusions*, New York, Monthly Review Press, 2002.

Kolko, Gabriel, *Confonting the Third World. United States Foreign Policy, 1945-1980*, New York, Pantheon Books, 1988.

L'Autre Amérique: les Américains contre l'état de guerre, ouvrage collectif, Paris, Textuel, 2002.

Le livre noir du capitalisme, ouvrage collectif, Paris, Le Temps des Cerises, 2002.

Lenin, V.I., *Imperialism, the Highest Stage of Capitalism. A popular outline*. Available on :http://www.marxists.org/archive/lenin/works/1916/imp-hsc/.

Lieven, Anatol, *America Right or Wrong: An Anatomy of American Nationalism*, Oxford, Oxford University Press, 2004.

Magdoff, Harry, *Imperialism Without Colonies*, New York, Monthly Review Press, 2003.

Mandel, Michael, *How America Gets Away With Murder. Illegal Wars, Collateral Damage and Crimes against Humanity*, London, Pluto Press, 2004.

Mayer, Arno, J., *The Furies: Violence and Terror in the French and Russian Revolutions*, Princeton, Princeton University Press, 2000.

Pauwels, Jacques, *The Myth of the Good War: America in the Second World War*, Halifax, James Lorimer & Company, Ltd, 2003.

Pelletière, Stephen, *Iraq and the International Oil System. Why America Went to War in the Gulf*, Washington, Maisonneuve Press, 2004.

Petras, James, Henry Veltmeyer, *Globalization Unmasked. Imperialism in the 21st Century*, London, Zed Books, 2001.

Petras, James, Henry Veltmeyer, *Empire with Imperialism*, London, Zed Books, 2005.

Petras, James, *The Power of Israel in the United States*, Atlanta, Clarity Press, 2006.

Preston Jr., William, Edward S. Herman, Herbert I. Schiller, *Hope and Folly: The United States and Unesco, 1945-1985*, Minneapolis, University of Minnesota Press, 1989.

Russell, Bertrand, *The Practice and Theory of Bolshevism*, London, Allen and Unwin, 1920 (reedited by Spokesman Books, Nottingham, 1995).

Russell, Bertrand, *Freedom and Organization, 1814-1914,* London, Routledge, 2001 (first edition, London, Allen and Unwin, 1934).

Said, Edward W., *The End of the Peace Process. Oslo and After*, New York, Vintage Books, 2001.

Simons, Geoff, *Targeting Iraq. Sanctions and Bombing in US Policy*, London, Saqi Books, 2002.

Index

Abu Ghraib, 145
Afghanistan, 54, 65–66, 85, 93, 95, 99;
  Rushdie and, 133; women in, 123–124
Africa, 54, 140
aggression, 43, 46–47, 94, 128
Albania, 92, 101
Albright, Madeline, 56
Algeria, 67
Allende, Salvador, 40, 47
alliances: Holy Alliance, 29, 31; between
  left and right, 155–156
allies, 164
altruism, 29–30, 32–33, 70–71
American Federation of Labor - Congress
  of Industrial Organizations (AFL-
  CIO), 144
"American gulag," 42
American holocaust, 37
Amerindians, 79
Amnesty International, 42, 147–149, 158–
  159
anti-Semitism, 108, 126
antiwar movements, 107, 128, 139, 144,
  153, 163; post-Vietnam, 131; solutions for Iraq by, 154–156; support of
  enemy by, 126–127
apartheid, 100
Arab world, 159–160
Arafat, Yasser, 107
Arbenz, Jacobo, 40, 58, 59, 96, 163
Argentina, 101
arguments against war, 91–106; anti-imperialist perspective on, 101–106;

defense of international law as, 93–
  101; weak, 91–93
armies, 67, 70–71, 114, 132
Aron, Raymond, 72
Asia, 54
assassination, 115, 116, 145
asylum, 76
Australia, 85
Avnery, Uni, 107

barricade effect, 42–52; Bosnia-
  Herzegovina and, 49–51; socialism
  and, 46–48; Soviet Union and, 42–46
Begin, Menahem, 107
Beinart, Peter, 120, 121
Belgium, 69
Berman, Paul, 120
Biden, Joseph, 153
Biko, Steve, 91
bin Laden, Osama, 95
Bissett, James
black people, 72–23
Blair, Tony, 137, 138, 142
Blum, William, 37
Boban, Mate, 49
Boer War, 29
"Al Bolivar" (Latin American television sta-
  tion), 159
Bolivia, 85
Bolsheviks, 48, 111
bombings, 69. *See also* weapons
Bosnia, 66, 67, 85
Bosnia-Hezegovina, 49–52

Bossuyt, Mark, 56
Brandt, Willy, 45–46
Brazil, 85
Brecht, Berthold, 87
Bremer, J. Paul, 132
Britain, 41, 54, 60, 144; colonialism and,
    69, 80, 81
British Guyana, 85
Brzezinski, Zbigniew, 54, 65
Bulgaria, 85
Burghardt, Jutta, 56
Bush, George H. W., 51, 67
Bush, George W., 44, 71, 73, 98, 125, 152;
    liberal supporters of, 119–122; loyal
    opposition and, 32; neither-nor stance
    and, 132; petitions regarding, 117–
    119; as radical liberal revolutionary,
    138; religion and, 31

Cambodia, 48, 93, 131
cantonization, 49–50
capitalism, 162–163; Cuba and, 85; deaths
    blamed on, 39; Guatemala and, 58
Carter, James A., 64, 65, 77, 172n3
Castro, Fidel, 47
casualties, 93, 99; deaths, 70, 137, 158–
    159, 178n2; in Fallujah, 144. See also
    mortality
Central America, 40, 92
Chalibi, Ahmed, 133
Chavez, Hugo, 105, 119, 163; media and,
    162; petitions regarding, 117; putsch
    against, 114–115
Chechnya, 79
children, 39, 40, 169n4
Chile, 40, 47, 85
China, 39, 52–53, 54, 77, 79
Chirac, Jacques, 87–88, 134, 174n29
Chomsky, Noam, 41, 151
civilians, 158–159
civil war in Iraq, 150, 153
Clinton, Bill, 51, 52, 63
Clinton, Hillary R., 153
Cold War, 43, 45–46, 61, 76, 119–120

collateral damages, 158
colonialism, 54, 113, 161, 164–165;
    Britain and, 69, 80, 81; deaths blamed
    on, 40; decolonization and, 35, 99,
    115; development and, 52, 74–75;
    human rights and, 69; neocolonialism
    and, 36, 54, 63, 113, 164; Rwanda
    and, 48
communism, 43, 115, 135; anticommu-
    nism and, 109; deaths blamed on, 39;
    demonization of term, 59; liberal intel-
    ligentsia and, 146; moral absolutism
    and, 133
Congo, 49, 69, 70
conservatives, 155
constitutions: European, 162; Iraqi, 147–149
consumption, 90
Contras, 102–104
Cooper, Marc, 62
cooperation, 140
costs of intervention, 35–60; barricade
    effect, 42–52; direct victims, 37–38;
    future risks, 52–58; in Guatemala, 58–
    60; killing hope, 38–42; in Nicaragua,
    36–37
crime. See international law
criminal justice, 146–147, 162
Croatia, 51
Cuba, 39–40, 47, 57, 76, 84–85, 97;
    embargo against, 84, 101
cultural revolution, 141
currency, 52
Curzon, Lord, 164, 180n25
Czechoslovakia, 92, 93, 110, 175n1

death. See mortality
death penalty, 113
debate, 32–33; rhetoric of support and,
    134–138
debt, 80, 101, 140
Declaration of Human Rights (1948), 72,
    76, 83
Declaration of Independence, U.S., 160
decolonization, 35, 99, 115

defense, 42–43, 45; armies and, 70–71; of democracy, 59; of Europe, 112–113; self-defense, 125; U.S. budget, 78, 173n19

defense of international law, 93–101; East Timor and, 99; government consent and, 94, 110; international order and, 95–97; non-aligned countries and, 97–98; U.S. and, 60, 98, 99–101

Democrats, 119

dependence on Third World countries, 52–55, 89, 113

Dershowitz, Alan M., 77

development, 73–83, 174n27; alternate paths to, 81–82, 83; colonialism and, 52, 74–75; construction of stable states and, 77–79; immigration and, 75–77; money flow and, 80–81; of Third World countries, 38–42

dictators, 37, 39, 47, 59, 95, 97

dominant powers, 162

domination, 37–38, 54, 55

Dominican Republic, 85

Downing Street memos, 124–126, 127

Drèze, Jean, 39

Dulles, Allen, 59

East Timor, 99

economic rights, 72, 80, 83, 84–85

economic systems, 100, 101

education, 53, 83, 100; in Cuba, 84–85

Eisenhower, Dwight, 60, 110

elections, 85, 104, 118, 119, 149

El Salvador, 68, 85, 115, 116

Elshtain, Jean Bethke, 122

embargoes, 97, 109; against Cuba, 84, 101; against Nicaragua, 102

emigration, 75–77

England, 54. See also Britain

entertainment, 53

Europe, 44, 53, 162, 163; as superpower, 112–115, 164–165

Euston Manifesto, 62–63

Fallaci, Oriana, 121

Fallujah, 70, 144–145, 149, 178n5

fanaticism, 60

fascism, 117; anti-fascism and, 107–112; "Islamo-fascism" and, 120–122; Nazism and, 43–45, 94, 107

First World War, 43, 48, 111–112

foreign aid budgets, 80

foreign policy, 172n3; AFL-CIO and, 144; of dominant governments, 111; of Europe, 113–114; Kerry and, 118

France, 60, 81, 102–103, 110, 114; antiwar movement in, 131; European constitution and, 162; far left in, 133–134; intelligentsia in, 64–65; invasion of Iraq and, 64; torture and, 67; Versailles Treaty and, 112; Vietnam and, 160

freedom: nation-building and, 78–79

freedom fighters, 103

freedom of expression, 31, 33

free press, 69–70

free will, 44

Friedman, Thomas L., 42, 121, 138

Frist, Bill, 156, 157

Garlasco, Mark E., 70

Gaza Strip, 76

Geneva Conventions, 147, 154

genocide, 55–56

Georgia, 85

Germany, 34, 81, 110, 175n1; Versailles Treaty and, 112

globalization, 38, 101

Gluckmann, André, 122

Good Fight, The (Beinart), 120

government, 78, 111; consent for war by, 94, 110; cooperation and, 140

Grenada, 100

Guatemala, 40, 52, 58–60, 85, 96

guerrilla forces, 67, 102, 157

Guevara, Che, 96

guilt weapon, 123–138; Afghan women and, 123–124; neither-nor stance and, 128–134; support of enemy and, 126–128; support rhetoric and, 134–138

Haiti, 76, 85
Halliday, Dennis, 55–56
Hamas, 128
Hammarskjöld, Dag, 60
Hari, Johann, 152, 179n12
Havel, Vaclav, 115–116, 121
health, 39, 46, 83, 86, 100, 140; in Cuba, 57, 84–85; in Iraq, 56
Herman, Edward S., 98
Hitchens, Christopher, 120
Hitler, Adolph, 29, 61, 93; "new Hitlers" and, 107, 109–110
Hobson, John, 54, 57–58
Ho Chi Minh, 96, 160–161
Holbrooke, Richard, 67–68, 153–154
Holy Alliance, 29, 31
Honduras, 59, 60
hope, 38–42, 161–165
human rights, 157–159, 161–162, 172n3; Declaration of Human Rights (1948), 72, 76, 83; International League of Human Rights, 99
Human Rights Commission, 97
Human Rights Watch, 158
human rights defenders, 61–90; armies and, 67, 70–71, 132; development of nations and, 73–83; free press and, 69–70; invasion of Iraq and, 61–64; national sovereignty and, 140; relationship of forces and, 88–90; rights prioritization of, 83–88; Soviet intervention in Afghanistan and, 65–66; torture and, 67, 68
Hurricane Katrina, 72–73
Hussein, Saddam, 56, 63, 125; antiwar movement and, 126–127; Iraqi constitution and, 149; mass graves and, 142–143; neither-nor stance and, 132; overthrow of, 163; rhetoric of support and, 137–138

idealism, 150, 154–155
ideology: power and, 29–34
Ignatieff, Michael, 41, 78–79

ignorance, 59
immigration, 75–77
"Imperialism Watch," 157–161
independence, 54
India, 39, 53, 54, 93
indigenous populations, 79, 81
individual rights, 72, 84
Indochina, 57
indoctrination mechanisms, 33
Indonesia, 85, 99
industrialization, 80–81
information battle, 139
insurrections, 68
internationalism, 115–117
international law, 49, 93–101; aggression and, 128; civil war justification and, 150; criminal justice and, 146–147, 162; East Timor and, 99; government consent and, 94, 110; Holbrooke and, 154; Hussein and, 138; international order and, 95–97; intervention and, 94–95; Israel and, 162; nation-building and, 78; non-aligned countries and, 97–98; U.S. and, 60, 98, 99–101; war on terror and, 93
International League of Human Rights, 99
international order, 95–97
interventions, 48–49, 94–95, 125; in Bosnia-Herzegovina, 49–52; low-intensity, 104; moderate, 72
invasions, 136; of Iraq, 61–64, 69–70, 114, 152, 154
Iran, 47, 56, 163
Iraq, 85, 93, 95, 144; Bremer's policy in, 132; Chalibi and, 133; Chomsky on, 151; civil war in, 150, 153; colonialism in, 164; constitution of, 147–149; France and, 134; hope for, 161; invasion of, 61–64, 69–70, 114, 152, 154; mass graves, 142–143; mortality and, 70, 137, 158–159; preventive war, 48; repairing damage in, 152, 153; resistance in, 136–137, 159; sanctions in, 55–56, 57; torture and, 67; vs. Yugoslavia, 111

Islamism, 43, 130-131, 146; Islamo-fascism and, 120-122
Israel, 40, 57, 76-77, 96, 126; human rights and, 69, 161-162; Al Jazeera and, 159; neither-nor stance and, 128; UN and, 100, 101
Italy, 85
Izetbegovic, Alija, 49-51, 67-68

Jamaica, 85
Japan, 81, 85
Al Jazeera (Arab television station), 159-160
Johnstone, Diana, 49
Judt, Tony, 122
justifiability, 43-45

Kagame, Paul, 49
Karadzic, Radovan, 49
Kennan, George, 46
Kerry, John, 117-119
Khmer Rouge, 48, 170n23
Khrushchev, Nikita, 46
Kirkpatrick, Jeane, 83, 174n25
Kosovo, 66, 92, 108, 110
Kouchner, Bernard, 57, 64, 67-68
Kuwait, 56, 136

labor, 52
Lancet, The (medical journal), 70
land reform, 39, 58
Lansing, Robert, 96
Laos, 85
Latin America, 39-40, 54, 105; economic and social rights in, 84; neocolonialism in, 163
leaders, 39
Lebanon, 69, 85, 107
legitimization, 32-33, 71; of Iraq occupations, 144-145, 147; preventive war against Hitler and, 108-112
Leopold II, king of Belgium, 69
liberalism, 87, 95, 109, 111, 119-122
liberation, 59

lies, 33-34
life expectancy, 39, 46. See also mortality
Lisbon Accord, 50-52
loyal opposition, 32

Mahathir, Mohamed, 83
Mandel, Michael, 93-94, 146
market, 42
Marx, Karl, 72
Marxism, 87
massacres, 49
mass graves, 142-143
materialism, 44
A Matter of Principle: Humanitarian Arguments for War in Iraq (Cushman), 61
Mayans, 58
media, 60, 69-70, 114, 131; Congo and, 49; European constitution and, 162; Hurricane Katrina and, 72-73; "Imperialism Watch" and, 159; Iraq occupation and, 144-145; propaganda, 69, 129-131, 141-143, 159, 178n5; respectability and, 129; secular priesthood and, 32; television and, 71, 159-160
military action, 66, 102, 125
military power, 104
Mill, John Stuart, 41
Milosevic, Slobodan, 132, 140
Minchnik, Adam, 121
Mitterrand, Francois, 67
modernization, 38-42, 40
money, 80
Mongolia, 85
Monroe Doctrine, 81
morality, 133, 150-152
mortality, 140, 178n2; children and, 39, 169n4; Iraq and, 70, 137, 158-159; life expectancy and, 39, 46
Mossadegh, Mohammed, 47, 163
Moynihan, Patrick, 99
Munich Agreement, 110

Nasser, Abdel, 107
national sovereignty, 117, 118-119, 128, 140

nation-building, 64, 78–79
nations, 97
natural resources, 54–55, 89–90
Nazism, 43–45, 94, 107
neither-nor stance 128–134
neocolonialism, 36, 54, 113, 163, 164
Nepal, 85
Neumann, Michael, 79
neutrality, 158
New Orleans, Louisiana, 151
Nicaragua, 36–37, 60, 85, 102–104, 119
Nixon, Richard M., 64
non-aligned countries, 97–98
non-governmental organizations (NGO), 146
North Atlantic Treaty Organization
      (NATO), 92, 110, 132
North-South relations, 140
Nuremburg, 94

objectives of war, 92
occupation of Iraq, 144–145, 147, 151
opposition, loyal, 32
oppression, 47
organizations in rich countries, 157–159
Owen, David, 51

pacifism, 112
Pakistan, 54
Palestine, 69, 76–77, 128, 154; anti-
      Semitism and, 126; Arab solidarity
      with, 160; human rights and, 162; Al
      Jazeera and, 159
Panama, 85
Paraguay, 101
Pascal, Blaise, 34
peace, 95
peace movements, 107, 128, 139, 144,
      153, 163; post-Vietnam, 131; solu-
      tions for Iraq by, 154–156; "support of
      enemy" by, 126–127
peace plans, 154
persecution, 76, 116
petitions, 117–119
petroleum, 52

Philippines, 85
Pinter, Harold, 37
policies, 35, 157; Cold War and, 45–46;
      Guatemala and, 52; human rights relat-
      ed, 67; against modernization, 40;
      nation-building, 64; of systematic
      domination, 37–38; terrorist attacks
      and, 44
political rights, 72, 80, 84, 86–87
Pol Pot, 48, 129, 131
Portugal, 85
poverty, 104, 140, 157; in Guatemala, 59;
      in Vietnam, 161
power, 65, 164–165; ideology and, 29–34;
      military, 104; stable states and, 77
preventive war, 48–49, 61; Bush adminis-
      tration and, 98; incompetent execution
      of, 121; international, 94; WWII and,
      108–112
priesthood, secular, 31, 32, 33
prisons, 67
progressive movements, 66, 105–106, 107,
      150; western obstruction of, 39–42
Project for a New American Century, 63
propaganda, 69, 129–131, 141–143, 159,
      178n5
protests, 66; antiwar demonstrations and,
      163; of human rights violations, 88–
      90; of Iraq occupation, 145
public health, 39, 57, 84–85. See also
      health
public opinion, 89, 129, 144; Afghanistan
      and, 133; world, 163
public school, 53

racism, 100, 105, 148
raw materials, 52, 140, 160
Rawnsley, Andrew, 138
reactions to aggression, 45, 46–47
Reagan, Ronald, 45, 83, 100, 103
refugees, 76
relationship of forces, 88–90, 150
religion, 31, 44; Islam, 43, 130–131, 146
respectability, 129

responsibility, 140, 150
Rhodes, Cecil, 75–76
rich countries, 72, 89, 157–159
rights: economic, 72, 80, 83, 84–85; individual, 72, 84; of Iraqis, 147–149; political, 72, 80, 84, 86–87; priorities between types of, 83–88; social, 72, 80, 83, 84–85
risks of Third World relations, 52–58
Roberts, Les, 70
Roosevelt, Kermit, 47
Roth, Kenneth, 158
rules of war, 146
Rumsfeld, Donald, 57
Rushdie, Salman, 133
Russel, Bertrand, 29, 45, 48, 96, 177n3
Russia, 45, 79, 85
Rwanda, 48, 49, 51, 140

Sabah, Ali, 149
Salisbury, Lord Robert Gascoyne-Cecil, 29, 31
sanctions, 55–56, 57, 69
Sandinistas, 36, 57, 102–104, 119
Sarajevo, 50
Schleisinger, Arthur, 29–30
school, 53
science, 53
Second World War, 108–112
secular priesthood, 31, 32, 33
Security Council of United Nations, 56, 60, 64, 125
self-defense, 125
Sen, Amartya, 39
September 11, 2001, 93; American reactions to, 42, 45; Arab reactions to, 168n7
Serbia, 80
Sharon, Ariel, 128
Sheehan, Cindy, 71
Sihanouk, Norodom, 48, 170n23
Slovakia, 85
socialism, 46–48, 85–86, 115, 133–134
social justice movements, 104

social rights, 72, 80, 83, 84–85
social security, 83
solidarity, 115
Somoza, 36
South, global, 141
sovereignty: absolute, 95; national, 117, 118–119, 128, 140
Soviet Union, 42–46, 61, 162; Afghanistan and, 65–66; Cold War policy in, 43; Cuba and, 84; Czechoslovakia and, 92, 93, 110; dominant ideology in, 31; German invasion of (1941), 34; industrialization and, 81
Spanish Republic, 110
Srebrenica, 48, 49
Stalin, Josef, 46, 129, 136–137
Stalinism, 43–45
standard of living, 82
Stead, William Thomas, 75–76
Suez Canal, 107
Sullivan, Andrew, 108
support, 124; active vs. passive, 126–128, 135; rhetoric of, 134–138
survival, 87
Swift, Jonathan, 34
Syria, 47

Taliban, 124, 157
Tallafar, 148
Telesur (Latin American television station), 159
television, 71, 159–160
Terror and Liberalism (Berman), 120
terrorism: demonization of term, 59; India and, 93; Iraqi resistance and, 160; Israel and, 77; justification for, 43–45; war on, 71, 93, 119–122
Third World, 35; cooperation and, 140; debt and, 80; dependence on, 52–55, 89, 113; development in, 38–42; international law and, 99; as political entity, 169n9; rhetoric of support and, 134
torture, 67, 68
totalitarian systems, 33

trade, 109
transition, 72
tribunals, 137, 145, 147, 168n2
Truman, Harry S, 60
Tunisia, 87–88

Uganda, 49
Ukraine, 85
United Fruit Company, 59
United Nations (UN), 96; Declaration of
    Human Rights (1948), 72, 76, 83; East
    Timor and, 99; Iraq sanctions and,
    55–56; Israel and, 100, 101; non-
    aligned countries and, 97–98; preven-
    tive war and, 110; Security Council of,
    56, 60, 64, 125; Srebenica and, 49;
    UNESCO and, 159; U.S. and, 60, 98,
    99–101
United States, 61, 162; "American gulag"
    and, 42; American holocaust and, 37;
    defense budget for, 78, 173n19;
    dependence on Third World of, 52–
    55; elections and, 85; Europe and,
    112–115; ideology in, 31; immigration
    and, 76; industrialization and, 81;
    international order and, 96; Nicaragua
    and, 36–37; public opinion in, 144; as
    sovereign nation, 95, 117, 118–119,
    128, 140; torture and, 67; UN and, 60,
    98, 99–101; victims of wars waged by,
    37–38; vs. world public opinion, 163;
    weapons proliferation and, 98
universalism, 162
Uzbekistan, 101

Venezuela, 104–105, 114–115, 117, 119,
    162
vengeance, 45
Versailles Treaty (1919), 43, 112, 170n14
Vickers, Michael, 123–124
Vietnam, 85, 93, 131, 160–161

Vietnam War, 64, 68, 131, 178n2; altruism
    and, 29–30; free press and, 69; ideolo-
    gy and, 34; liberal intelligentsia and,
    146; neither-nor stance and, 129; tor-
    ture and, 67
violence, 70, 77, 163; domination and, 55;
    genocide and, 55–56; massacres and,
    49; revolutionary, 47; in Soviet Union,
    43. See also casualties
vision of the world, 139–150
Voltaire, François-Marie Arouet de, 131
Von Sponeck, Hans, 56

Walzer, Michael, 62, 122
war, 79; of aggression, 94; of all against all,
    95; Boer War, 29; Cold War, 43, 45–
    46, 61, 76, 119–120; preventive, 48–
    49, 61, 94, 98, 108–112, 121; against
    terror, 71, 93, 119–122; WWI, 43, 48,
    111–112; WWII, 108–112. See also
    Vietnam War
weak arguments, 91–93
weapons, 54, 95, 171n31; of mass destruc-
    tion, 61, 63, 64, 71, 78, 98, 125;
    nuclear, 100, 163, 175n7; proliferation
    of, 98
Weisberg, Jacob, 121
West, Kayne, 72–73
Western Left, 66
Will, George, 68
Wilson, Woodrow, 96
women, 123–124, 131
World War I, 43, 48, 111–112
World War II, 108–112

Xiaoping, Deng, 77

Young, Hugo, 137, 138
Yugoslavia, 50–51, 79, 80, 85, 111

Zimmermann, Warren, 50

CPSIA information can be obtained at www.ICGtesting.com
Printed in the USA
BVOW071934260712

296289BV00001B/18/P